EVELYN WAUGH

LITERATURE AND LIFE:
BRITISH WRITERS

Selected list of titles:

Complete list of titles in the series available from the publisher on request. Some titles are also in paperback.

EVELYN WAUGH

Katharyn W. Crabbe

A Frederick Ungar Book

CONTINUUM • NEW YORK

4647843

1988

The Continuum Publishing Company
370 Lexington Avenue
New York, NY 10017

Copyright © 1988 by Katharyn W. Crabbe

Printed in the United States of America

Library of Congress Cataloging-in-Publication Data

Crabbe, Katharyn W., 1945–
Evelyn Waugh.

16.95

(Literature and life. British writers)
Bibliography: p.
Includes index.
1. Waugh, Evelyn, 1903–1966. 2. Novelists, English—
20th century—Biography. I. Title. II. Series.
PR6045.A97Z628   1988   823'.912 [B]   87-13927
ISBN 0-8044-2107-2

55931

For Lynn and Laura

Contents

Chronology

1903   Born to Arthur and Catherine Waugh, October 28.

1910   Enters Heath Mount School as a day student.

1914   World War I begins.

1917   Enters Lancing College.

1919   Introduced to Francis Crease.

1922   Enters Hertford College, Oxford University.

1924   Leaves Oxford without completing his degree. Studies art in London.

1925   Becomes a schoolmaster.

1927   Marries Evelyn Gardner.

1928   Publishes *Rossetti: His Life and Works* and *Decline and Fall.*

1929   Divorced.

1930   Publishes *Vile Bodies* and *Labels*. Converts to Catholicism. Travels to Ethiopia for the coronation of Haile Selassie.

1931   Publishes *Remote People*.

1932   Publishes *Black Mischief*. Begins travels in South America.

1933   Returns from South America. Meets Laura Herbert.

1934   Publishes *Ninety-Two Days* and *A Handful of Dust*.

1935   Publishes *Edmund Campion*, which wins Hawthornden Prize. Travels to Ethiopia as a war correspondent.

1936   Publishes *Waugh in Abyssinia*.

1937   Marries Laura Herbert. Establishes residence at Piers Court, Gloustershire.

1938   Publishes *Scoop*. Daughter Teresa born. Travels to Mexico.

1939   Publishes *Robbery Under Law*. Son Auberon born. Joins Marines.

1941   Publishes "My Father's House," which later becomes *Work Suspended*. Participates in battle of Crete.

1942   Publishes *Put Out More Flags*. Daughter Margaret born. Trains as Commando.

1944   Posted to Yugoslavia. Daughter Harriet born. *Brideshead Revisited* published privately.

1945   Publishes *Brideshead Revisited*.

1946   Travels to Spain. Publishes *When the Going Was Good*. Son
       James born.

1947   Publishes *Scott-King's Modern Europe*. Travels to Los Angeles.

1948   Publishes *The Loved One*.

1950   Publishes *Helena*. Son Septimus born.

1952   Publishes *Men at Arms*.

1953   Publishes *Love Among the Ruins*.

1954   Suffers nervous breakdown while on cruise.

1955   Publishes *Officers and Gentlemen*. Sues Nancy Spain and the
       Daily Express. Contributes to *Noblesse Oblige* with Nancy
       Mitford.

1956   Moves to Combe Florey, Somerset.

1957   Publishes *The Ordeal of Gilbert Pinfold*. Ronald Knox dies.

1958   Travels to Africa.

1959   Publishes *Monsignor Ronald Knox*.

1960   Publishes *Tourist in Africa*.

1961   Publishes *Unconditional Surrender*. Does Wodehouse broad-
       cast on BBC.

1962   Travels to British Guiana with daughter Margaret.

1963   Publishes *Basil Seal Rides Again*.

1964   Publishes *A Little Learning*.

1966   Dies at home on Easter Sunday, April 10.

1

Biography

In *The Ordeal of Gilbert Pinfold,* a frankly autobiographical novel published when he was fifty-four-years old, Evelyn Waugh gave posterity a good indication of how he saw his own achievement and how he hoped to be remembered. He placed himself in the tradition of "artists and craftsmen of the late eighteenth century" and noted that, like them, the "English novelists of the present day" represent a period in which "there was so much will and so much ability to please." He pointed out that his books were not so much statements of "cosmic significance" as "objects which he had made." He was proud of them without being vain about them. There were none he wanted to disown but some he would like to revise.[1] The analysis seems honest and not self-aggrandizing; the aspirations seem modest and worthwhile. An author of more sanguine temperament who had written the books and articles Waugh wrote and who had tested them against Waugh's touchstones might have died a happy man.

When Waugh died at home on Easter Sunday in 1966, however, obituaries throughout the world observed that the witty young man of letters who had celebrated (and some said, invented) the "bright young things" of English society in the twenties had become crotchety, misanthropic, unhappy, and, worse, serious in his last years. The attacks in the obituaries were so vicious, in fact, that his son felt that he had to register a public objection.[2] To be sure, Waugh was uncomfortable in the 1960s: he disapproved of Labour governments and their taxation policies; he deplored the changes taking place in the Catholic church, particularly in the liturgy; and he feared that he was nearing the end of the road as a novelist. The vicissitudes of life and a history of overindulgence in food, alcohol, and sleeping drafts had undermined his health and seemingly eradicated any patience he ever had with those who disagreed with him. Yet there were those who fondly remembered when his wit was as sharp, if less caustic; his opinions as conservative, if less petulantly expressed; and his habits as irregular, if less self-damaging. For those who loved him, there seemed to have been less change in him than met the eye.

Accounts of Waugh's childhood vary little in their opinions that it was happy, almost idyllic. It is certainly safe to say that it was comfortable. His father, Arthur Waugh, was a senior editor of Chapman and Hall, a London publishing company, and an essayist and reviewer himself. The elder Waugh was successful enough in his profession to build a home in a village just outside London and to belong to a club called the Savile. He and his wife were able to provide nurses for his two sons when they were young and to send them to good public schools when they grew older.

Alec, the elder child in the family, was five years old when his younger brother was born in the fall of 1903. The baby was christened Arthur Evelyn St. John Waugh, the Evelyn being a result of "a whim" on the part of his mother.[3] With five years between them, the two boys seem not to have been playmates or close companions. Evelyn Waugh remarks in his autobiography that "the five years that separated us made, in childhood, a complete barrier."[4]

In addition to being comfortable, Waugh's childhood was markedly ordinary. His autobiography is sprinkled with accounts of the activities of an interesting, busy, and indulged younger son—rabbit hutches are built, novels are written, a neighborhood club is formed. And it seems clear from his own account that language unfailingly assumed the central place in the early home life of the young Waugh.

Arthur Waugh, after all, was not only an editor; he was a friend and supporter of fledgling writers and an associate and friend of many established men of letters as well as an active writer of essays and reviews himself. Evenings at the Waugh household often featured Arthur Waugh reading aloud from the classic poems or plays of English literature, from which his son developed a keen sense of the rhythms and cadences of the language. When Waugh acknowledged his abiding interest in style in 1946, he attributed it to his father, saying, "My father, who was a respected literary critic of his day, first imbued me with the desire to learn this language, of which he had a mastery."[5]

In the earliest surviving example of Waugh's writing, "The Curse of the Horse Race," written in 1910 when he was six years old, one can perceive the beginnings of the clarity and ironic tone that came to be Waugh's trademark.

I bet you 500 pounds I'll win. The speaker was Rupert a man of about 25 he had a dark bushy mistarsh and flashing eyes. I should not trust to much on your horse said Tom for indeed he had not the sum to spear.[6]

The rhythm of the lines and the barb about Tom's finances in the final tag are plainly superior to the spelling and punctuation, and suggest either a sophisticated sense of literary conventions or an understanding of the complexity of human behavior disconcerting in one so young.

The second major force in Waugh's youngest years was religion. The family was consistent but not compulsive about religious observance, and Waugh recalls of his father that "he liked church-going with a preference for colorful and ceremonious services and never missed a Sunday, usually attending whatever place was nearest, irrespective of its theological complexion. . . . In my childhood my father read family prayers every morning."[7] As a little boy, he was also extremely fond of his nurse, whose evangelical bent made religion central to her own life and also to that of her charge.

The nearest church, for the years of Waugh's early adolescence, was Anglican, located in the village of Hamstead, and served by a colorful and eccentric vicar. The boy, passing through a phase of piety, became intrigued by the ceremony of the high-church celebration of the eucharist and eventually became an altar boy. He also constructed an altar in his bedroom, complete with a brass tray for burning incense.

This interest in religion and its rituals came to occupy an important position in Waugh's life, not only because it marked the beginning of his sense of the importance of the "supernatural" or the "mysterious" but also because it determined eventually the choice of his public school and the breaking of a family tradition. The chain of events started with Waugh's older brother, Alec.

Alec Waugh attended Sherbourne, the public school in which Arthur Waugh had been educated and which, it was assumed, his younger son would also attend. Alec was apparently in and out of trouble often at Sherbourne and was ultimately expelled. Soon after leaving the school, he published his first novel, *The Loom of Youth*, which described, as Waugh puts it, ". . . his schooldays with a realism that was then unusual."[8] Because the book was clearly a thinly disguised autobiography, and because it acknowledged the existence at Sherbourne of hazing, bullying and homosexual attachments (common, one believes, at all similar schools as well, but not something anyone cared to recognize), the administrators and trustees of the school were furious. Both Alec and his father were struck from the alumni list of Sherbourne, and Arthur Waugh found himself with a second son of public-school age and no school to which to send him.

Apparently motivated at least to some degree by the younger Waugh's piety and interest in the trappings of religion, Arthur Waugh sent Evelyn to Lancing, a small public school "designed to inculcate Highchurchmanship."[9] Waugh's earliest diaries, written at Lancing between 1914 and 1916, suggest that his religious interests continued for some time, and that those interests combined with interests in language, graphic arts, and architecture as he matured.

At home and at school, Waugh was always a writer and was always concerned about his audience's reception of his work. His interest in publication probably first developed from his success in designing covers for Chapman and Hall publications: "it is so priceless getting one's things printed," he wrote in his diary.[10] Actually, it was not priceless at all; the price was a guinea (twenty-one shillings) and most of the proceeds were spent on the artist's library. But the excitement of the publication was probably as important as the money, and it contributed to Waugh's growing tendency to celebrate himself: "In the last generation," he wrote, "people never began to think until they were about nineteen, to say nothing of thinking about publishing books and pictures."[11]

At Lancing, Waugh was able to develop his talent as a graphic artist as well as his verbal skills. Through the head of his dormitory he met Francis Crease, an artist with a consuming interest in calligraphy. Crease greeted Waugh's first lesson for him by noting "you have just written the most beautiful *E* since the Book of Kells."[12] As a part of his attempt to merge his religious interests with all other aspects of his life, Waugh had begun to make illuminations, decorated manuscripts of religious or devotional subjects in which the first capital letter and the margins of the page are ornamented. Although he was primarily interested in the ornamentation, he saw at once that Crease had much to teach him about lettering, and he was clever enough to try to learn it.

A second important influence at Lancing was J. F. Roxburgh, the classics master. From him Waugh learned to value above all else precise and cliche-free language and to question the logical bases of all assertions, including the tenets of Christianity. By the time he left Lancing, the pious boy who had

been at pains to build a shrine complete with a crucifix and
". . . two sweet brass bowls to fill with flowers,"[13] had become
a self-styled agnostic.

The loss of his youthful faith, although significant, was not
the most important experience of Waugh's life at Lancing. More
important are the activities he undertook and the roles he assumed in an effort to become first an accepted member, and
later a leader, of his group. Gaining acceptance seems to have
been a painful process for Waugh, perhaps partly because he
had never lived away from home before going to Lancing and
was thus accustomed to always being at the center of a family.
Certainly part of the problem was that he entered Lancing in
midyear, after the other boys had already made friends, established pecking orders, and created social circles. Only one other
boy entered the school when he did, and they were friends in
exile for two terms until the next set of new boys appeared and
promoted them to members of the established order. The lonely
process of working one's way into the social world may well be
at the root of Waugh's recurrent concern with the fate of exiles
in his novels.

Having survived two terms of relative isolation, Waugh
eventually became an accepted member of his group. Although
he was never very successful at athletics, he participated in box-
ing, swimming, and running. He rose to the position of house
captain, and he helped to establish a debating society called the
Dilettanti, in which he headed the art group. He wrote the
Prize Poem in his last year and won the English Literature Prize.
These achievements marked his adjustment to Lancing, his acceptance of his role, and his acceptability to his peers. Even
when success came, however, Waugh was easily bored and eager to move on, out of his public school and on to a university.
The diaries of his last months at Lancing are a chorus of com-
plaints about the dreariness of his present life and the promise
of the future.

In the years between the two wars, publishing had not prospered, and Waugh realized that although his education was not endangered, it would be a strain on his father's resources. He thus resolved to try for the biggest scholarship available to him. It was not, as his father had hoped, a scholarship to New College but to Hertford College, a respectable but not very prominent unit of Oxford University. Waugh won the scholarship and set off for Oxford, as he had for Lancing, in the middle of the year.

Oxford was for Waugh what it was for many young men in the years immediately following the first World War: gray and gold, a place in which to grow up and a place to make discoveries (not all of them academic or even intellectual). In both *Decline and Fall* and *Brideshead Revisited* traces of Waugh's Oxford experience can be found, with its teas of honey buns and anchovy toast, its elaborate luncheons, and its dangerous rooms on the ground floor which provided a natural gathering place for one's friends. There were athletes and aesthetes, Oxford Union orators, and a wide range of dons and tutors. Ostensibly, Waugh went to Oxford to study history, but in reality he went there to experience what Oxford had to offer, and he took in as much as he could.

By Waugh's own admission, he was not much of a student at Oxford. The system, which provided much freedom and thus demanded much responsibility, was one that played into the hands of the arrogant young who were sure they could make up in weeks what they had neglected for years. Perhaps Waugh was unfortunate in being assigned to a tutor who did not live up to his expectations—C.R.M.F. Cruttwell was certainly not the tutor the young man had hoped for—but even Waugh later admitted that he simply was not interested in being educated at the time. So he insulted Cruttwell, teased him as Sebastian and Charles teased Mr. Samgrass in *Brideshead Revisited,* and finished by not knowing much more about history when he left Oxford than he had when he entered.

Nonetheless, no one could say that Waugh's years at Oxford were wasted. Although he had no idea of the profession for which he was preparing, he was learning much that was eventually to be of use. Instead of studying history, he entertained friends and was entertained by them. He spoke before the Oxford Union (an undergraduate debating society), he wrote for several publications loosely associated with the university, and in general he lived beyond his means. The last required him to take up cigar smoking, to drink beer and wine, and to dine out regularly with friends. He spent a pleasant if rather dissipated three years before taking the exams that were to lead to a degree in history. Unable to compensate for two-and-one-half years of ignoring his reading in a single term, he passed at the third-class level, and both he and his father were so disgusted with the performance that Waugh returned home without putting in the one additional term that would have earned him the degree.

Leaving Oxford, Waugh went through a lonely and rather chaotic late adolescence. He attended art school, but dropped out when he discovered he was more interested in parties than painting. Waugh wrote to Harold Acton:

I have practically decided that it is impossible to draw in London between tube journeys and telephone calls and am seriously considering going to live in Sussex with a man called James Guthrie who has a printing press where he is making books from copper plates. [14]

Having investigated Guthrie's facility and having discovered that the printing was really being done by photographic processes rather than by copper plates, Waugh decided not to go to Sussex. On January 5, 1925, he confided to his diary that Mr. Banks of Arnold House "is going to pay me £160 to teach little boys for him for a year. I think this will be bloody but most useful to a man as poor as I." [15]

In June of 1925, Alec Waugh suggested that his brother might be a suitable secretary to C. K. Moncrieff, the translator of Proust's *Remembrance of Things Past*. On the strength of this recommendation, Waugh resigned his position at Arnold House, and when the Moncrieff job fell through, he was unemployed again. Through a friend, Richard Greene, he secured a position at Aston Clinton in a school for problem boys (the diaries of the period note, "Taught lunatics," and "Taught the poor mad boys"), where he instructed until he was fired in 1927 either for drunkenness, or for trying to seduce one of the matrons.[16]

Waugh must have felt that he was on the down-hill track when he left Aston Clinton; in the diary he complains of his next position, "The school in Notting Hill is quite awful. All the masters drop their aitches and spit in the fire and scratch their genitals."[17] By May of 1927, however, Duckworth's had given him a two-hundred pound advance on a biography of Dante Gabriel Rossetti, and he had a temporary position at the *Daily Express*. The *Express* job lasted only a few weeks, but by that time he had begun his first commercially published work, *Rossetti: His Life and Works*. The book met with critical although not popular acclaim. But it was important to Waugh because it was the first unattenuated success he had achieved since leaving Lancing.

At this point in Waugh's life, some kind of symbolic achievement was especially important, for he had met a woman he wanted to marry. Evelyn Gardner, daughter of the first Baron Barghclere, became Waugh's wife in a secret ceremony on June 27, 1928. In their families, no one seemed very pleased; Evelyn Gardner's mother was actively opposed to her daughter's marrying a young man of few accomplishments and fewer prospects. By September of that year, however, both his prospects and his accomplishments had improved. He had published his first novel, *Decline and Fall*.

Decline and Fall and the Rossetti biography were fairly successful and gave Waugh a sufficient reputation so that he was able to find more opportunities for the journalistic writing that was to be, for many years, an important source of income. His journalism also helped keep his name before the public and, in a way, led to the first of a number of travel books that were to become central to his creative life. Thinking that a journey to the Mediterranean would be good for his young and ill wife (apparently she had a viral infection from which she was slow to recover), Waugh instructed his agent to arrange inexpensive passage. The agent did better than that, arranging free passage on the Norwegian ship M. Y. *Stella Polaris*. In exchange for the passage, Waugh was to publicize the line in the articles he had been commissioned to write. The articles and travel notes were later reworked into *Labels* (1930), his first travel book.

The Stella Polaris trip in February 1929 was a financial success but a personal failure. Ill when she left England, Waugh's wife was hospitalized with double pneumonia in Haifa, and he went on his social rounds without her. When they returned to London, Waugh went to the country to work on his second novel, *Vile Bodies*. While he was away, his wife, now recovered, fell in love with John Heygate, a young man from the BBC. Although the two Evelyns attempted a reconciliation, their brief marriage was over, and Waugh fell into a state of bitter despair.

Waugh's dominant emotion, to judge by his letters, was not sadness nor anger, but humiliation. He was deeply hurt by the rejection, but seemed to be just as hurt by "the fact that she should have chosen a ramshackle oaf like Heygate."[18] And it was no doubt a blow to a young man who had just become a literary lion to have to write home to ask his parents, "May I come and live with you sometimes?"[19]

Although the marriage was a failure, *Vile Bodies* was a great success. It was far more widely discussed and reviewed than *Decline and Fall*, and Waugh was remarking with some glee in May of 1930 that a monthly stipend of thirty pounds from the *Daily Mail* ". . . brings my regular income temporarily up to about £2,500 a year."[20]

Desperately unhappy for the first time in his adult life, Waugh seems to have sought comfort in the Christian faith he had abandoned at Lancing. However, he did not return to the Anglican church but began instead to take instruction in Catholicism. Whether it was his study of history or the temper of the times that tipped the balance, he was convinced that, if one true faith existed, it must be Roman Catholic, for the Protestant religions were clearly offshoots. Father Martin D'Arcy was the instructor, and by the end of September 1930, he judged his student ready to be received into the church. This event was one of the most significant and positive in Waugh's life; his religion determined when he would be married and to whom, how he would educate his children and, ultimately, what he would take as his subject matter. Although he later took issue with some of the reforms of Vatican II, he seems never to have wavered in his conviction that Catholicism was the one true faith.

In October, a year after entering the church, Waugh took the advice of his old friend Alastair Graham to travel to Abyssinia, now Ethiopia, for the coronation of Haile Selassie. This journey was the source of the second travel book *Remote People* and through it the source of the novel *Black Mischief*. *Black Mischief* was well received, with the exception of the review in the Catholic weekly, *The Tablet*, where the reviewer attacked the book not for its weaknesses as fiction but for its imperfections in morality. Despite the denunciations of *The Tablet*, however, the novel sold well. But even before its run was established, the footloose Waugh was on his way to Brazil and British Guiana.

This journey, which occupied the months of December 1932 through April 1933, eventually yielded up another travel book, *Ninety-two Days*, and a wonderful short story, "The Man Who Liked Dickens," which became the central episode of his next novel, *A Handful of Dust*. Soon after his return to England in the spring of 1933, Waugh journeyed to Italy where he met Laura Herbert, whom he later married.

A Handful of Dust, which appeared in 1934, was received as Waugh's best novel to date, and for many readers it has retained that distinction.[21] Historically, it is of some interest because in it Waugh dealt for the first time with the theme of marital infidelity and its effects, turning to fictional ends the most unpleasant experience of his young life as he had already turned many more positive experiences.

Waugh's next book *Edmund Campion* (1935), was a biography of the great English martyr and saint. As his first book on a religious subject, *Edmund Campion* met with widely varied critical responses. For Graham Greene, "Mr. Waugh's study [was] a model of what a short biography should be."[22] For J. A. Kensit, "Evelyn Waugh's book . . . merely served up afresh the discredited Jesuit history of Campion."[23] And for the most cynical, it was a ploy to curry favor with the Catholic hierarchy and so hasten the decision on Waugh's application for the annulment of his first marriage which would allow him to marry Laura Herbert.

It is probable that none of these perspectives is wholly correct. What is beyond dispute is that the book is a moving apologia for the Catholic position during the reign of Elizabeth I and that it is a sensitive depiction of the life of the saint. In 1935, *Edmund Campion* was awarded the Hawthornden Prize as the best Catholic book of the year. Regarded dispassionately, the book is one of Waugh's weaker works, so it seems ironic that public approbation should accrue more to Campion than to *A Handful of Dust* or *The Loved One*.

Also in 1935, Waugh left England once again for Abyssinia where war with Italy was expected to break out immediately. From the ensuing chaotic experiences there emerged *Waugh in Abyssinia*, a book that the author had wanted to call *The Disappointing War*. He was not, in the true sense of the term, a war correspondent, but he had been to Abyssinia before to witness the crowning of the Emperor Haile Selassie, and as he observed, "anyone who had actually spent a few weeks in Abyssinia itself, and had read the dozen or so books which constituted the entire English bibliography of the subject, might claim to be an expert."[24] Waugh indeed did this.

By the end of 1936, Waugh was back in England with the manuscript of *Waugh in Abyssinia* and a new novel, *Scoop*, underway. On April 17, 1937, he married Laura Herbert with whom he settled down at a country home called Piers Court near Stinchcomb in Gloucestershire. The novel was nearly finished by the end of the year and it came out in May of 1938, shortly after the birth of their first child, Teresa.

In May of 1938, Waugh was also asked by Clive Pearson ("a very rich chap [who] wants me to write a book about Mexico,"[25]) to travel to that country and observe the effects of the recent nationalization of foreign holdings. The result was *Robbery Under Law*, published in June 1939, probably the least successful of any Waugh book. Not only did it not sell, it was not even a *succès d'estime*, and in later years Waugh dismissed it saying, "I am content to leave [it] in oblivion, for it dealt little with travel and much with political questions."[26]

By this time, the British were at war and Waugh had determined to seek active service, although he knew that his age (he was thirty-six) would make it difficult for him to find an assignment appropriate for the hero he meant to be. After a great deal of trouble, he managed to secure a commission in the Royal Marines. The adventures of his fictional characters in *Put Out More Flags* and the *Sword of Honour* trilogy follow his own career closely. Like Cedric Lyne, he became battalion intelligence officer and later, like Peter Pastmaster and his friends, he transferred to Combined Operations or "Commando." With the Commandos he fought in Crete as part of the rear guard. Like Alastair and Sonia, he and Laura lived in hotels and villas near his training areas, and like Cedric he participated in a bizzare embarkation on a Pacific and Orient cruise ship that had been converted to a troopship. In the interval, Laura gave birth to their eldest son, Auberon, and Waugh began work on a new novel, *Work Suspended*. But events moved too fast. He was unable to finish the novel before the world changed irrevocably, and the fragment did not appear until 1942, by which time the Waughs had been blessed with a second daughter and third child, Margaret.

After he abandoned *Work Suspended*, Waugh began a new novel, *Put Out More Flags*, which was written, he said, to dispel the gloom in the belly of a troopship. Familiar characters from earlier novels reappear—Basil Seal, Sir Joseph Mainwaring, Alastair Digby-Vane-Trumpington—but they have mellowed and become much less self-centered. Yet, the old manic sense of fun is there, even in the face of war and the difficulties of being too old to be useful and too young to be content to stay at home.

Reading Waugh's war novels, one might think that he had been a total failure as a military man. This is not quite the case, although some episodes in his military career come rather close to supporting that thesis. It appears that Waugh did not submit to discipline very readily and that consequently he sometimes devoted considerable energy to revealing to the military its own lunacy. On the other hand, there seems to be no question at all of his personal bravery or his patriotism. He joined the Royal Marines when he could have remained a civilian; he sought combat duty when he could have disappeared into the bureaucracy; and he acquitted himself respectably when he actually faced combat on Crete and in Yugoslavia.

Even in the midst of the war, Waugh never relinquished his identity as a novelist. One of his greatest contretemps with military authority involved the conflicting claims of his military duty and his art, for when he began to work on the novel that was to become *Brideshead Revisited*, he quickly realized that unlike *Put Out More Flags*, *Brideshead* could not be written on a troopship. Instead he would need an extended period (at least three months) of solitude and concentrated effort to give the idea form. There were categories of artistic activity that were thought to contribute to the war effort, but Waugh was honest enough to admit in his request for leave that the novel he proposed to write would not have "any immediate propaganda value."[27] Partially for this reason and partially because he had an uncanny instinct for alienating those who were less quick than he, especially if they were in authority, the War Office was reluctant to grant him leave. In fact, even though they really had no duty for which he was needed, they repeatedly tried to assign him tasks ranging from aide-de-camp to a major general to assistant registrar at a hospital.[28] He managed to avoid all the snares and to complete *Brideshead* by mid-June of 1944, one month after the birth of his third daughter, Harriet.

This book was important to Waugh for reasons both artistic and pragmatic. He knew that *Brideshead Revisited* was a departure—the point of view had shifted, the themes were new, and it was not "meant to be funny"—and he thought it was very good. As early as April 1944 he was referring to the *Magnum Opus* in letters to his agent. And after the private edition was circulated, he wrote to Nancy Mitford to confess, "For the first time since 1928, I am eager about a book."[29]

Financially, *Brideshead Revisited* was a huge success both in the United Kingdom and in the United States, and 1945 found Waugh contemplating the congenial chore of sheltering royalty income. He complains, and here we begin to hear a new note, that there is no advantage in earning more than five-thousand pounds per year "under the present regime."[30]

When the war ended and Waugh returned to England to resume life as a novelist and a family man, his literary output lessened for a period. He commenced a study of the life of St. Helena that he soon abandoned. He also started "a novel of school life in 1919," which his biographer describes as having disappeared completely but which must be the fragment "Charles Ryder's Schooldays," published in *Charles Ryder's Schooldays and Other Stories*, 1982. He kept his name before the public, however, by bringing out in 1946 a collection of previously published travel pieces (*When the Going Was Good*) and, inspired by a trip to Spain, *Scott-King's Modern Europe* in 1947. In June of 1946, his second son, James, was born.

Despite serious misgivings and a well-placed mistrust of the movie magnates, Waugh agreed in 1947 to travel to Hollywood to discuss a possible film version of *Brideshead Revisited*. It appears that Waugh was not really very sanguine about the idea, so he could accept MGM's withdrawal from the project with equanimity. In any case, both he and Laura enjoyed the society of Los Angeles and the "effortless luxury" in which they were maintained. More important, they discovered Forest Lawn Cemetery and there Waugh found a "jolly setting" for a story about "the Anglo-American cultural impasse."[31] Generations of readers have come to agree with him that the story thus described, *The Loved One*, is one of his great comic successes.

Although he had earlier given up a project on the life of St. Helena, Waugh returned to the subject in the late forties, this time with the intention of making it a historical novel. He seems to have realized that there was every possibility that *Helena* would not be successful, as he complained to Nancy Mitford several times that even though the book would be a masterpiece, "No one will like it at all."[32] But Waugh worked at it, and in the summer of 1950, about the same time that his youngest child, Septimus, was born, *Helena* appeared. Waugh wrote to John Betjeman, "I liked Helena's sanctity because it is in contrast to all that moderns think of as sanctity. She wasn't thrown to the lions, she wasn't a contemplative, she wasn't poor & hungry, she didn't look like an El Greco. She just discovered what it was God had chosen for her to do and did it."[33]

After *Helena*, Waugh commenced work on a novel he described for Nancy Mitford as "unreadable & endless."[34] Although he saw the resulting *Men at Arms* as but one volume of a trilogy (sometimes a quartet), he was still disappointed in the reception.

After the moderate reception of *Men at Arms*, Waugh was further depressed by the even-more-negative response to his short novel, *Love Among the Ruins* (1953). This futuristic fantasy, which has been described as "a short nightmare on the socialist state," was, in Waugh's words, "hastily finished & injudiciously published."[35] The reviewers agreed with his assessment.

During the next few years as Waugh's hearing deteriorated

and rheumatism and insomnia drove him to increased use of chloral, a sleeping medicine, his mental well-being also deteriorated. In an attempt to establish some productive work habits, he embarked alone on a voyage to Ceylon. He wrote to his daughter, Margaret, "I shant [sic] come back until I have finished my book [*Officers and Gentlemen*, 1955], but I hope I shall do that on the voyage."[36] Instead of soothing him, as he had hoped, the trip resulted in Waugh's becoming increasingly alienated and finally convinced that a group of "psychologists" on board the ship were spying on everything he said or thought or read, and that they had wired his stateroom so that they could torment him by whispering back to him every word he uttered. Ultimately, his wife pursuaded him to fly back to England and to consult an "alienist." The diagnosis: hallucinations brought on by the combination of alcohol and the narcotic drugs he used as sleeping drafts. It was a painful and difficult episode for Waugh, but from it he was able to gather the seeds of *The Ordeal of Gilbert Pinfold*, a novel that follows its author's misadventures closely.

Unlike his hero, however, Waugh completed the work in progress before proceeding to write *The Ordeal of Gilbert Pinfold*. Thus, the first novel to appear after his return from his voyage was *Officers and Gentlemen*, which came out in June 1955. The publication of this novel led to one of the most extravagent and amusing episodes of Waugh's public life—the episode involving Nancy Spain.

Nancy Spain was the chief reviewer on the *Daily Express* at the time *Officers and Gentlemen* appeared. She arrived at Waugh's home one day, accompanied by Lord Noel-Buxton, insisting that Waugh submit to an interview. He refused and sent them away, adding insult to injury by writing a very funny article about the episode for the *Spectator*. It begins "I'm not on business. I'm a member of the House of Lords,"[37] and then harshly satirizes both of his would-be interviewers. Less than a year later, in the course of excoriating the reviews of John Wain, Waugh wrote that "The Beaverbrook press [of which Nancy Spain was a mem-

ber] is no longer listed as having any influence at all."[38] This
nettled Miss Spain who then wrote a response implying that
Evelyn Waugh was not as good a novelist as his brother, Alec;
that he was jealous of his brother's success; and that the success
of his brother's most recent novel, *Island in the Sun*, was directly
attributable to her review.

Waugh, who always read the papers carefully for anything
that could be construed as libelous, spotted Nancy Spain's inju-
dicious remarks. Concerned as he always was about money and
the costs of educating his children, Waugh was delighted over
the possibility of suing Nancy Spain and the Beaverbrook Press
for tax-free money. On the advice, also, of his lawyers Waugh
sued, asserting that her remarks implied that he was a writer of
little talent whose stories, books, and film scripts were not worth
buying and whose name had no importance to the general public. He won and collected two thousand pounds in addition to
his costs. Furthermore, Nancy Spain was indiscrete enough to
review a book which attacked Waugh and to quote some of the
most hostile comments while the libel case was waiting to come
to court. As a consequence, he again threatened to sue, and
settled out of court for another three thousand pounds.

At about the time the Nancy Spain episode began, Waugh
grew to be seriously unhappy over the real-estate development
of the area surrounding his home in Gloucestershire. In July of
1956, he and his family found a new home in the west country,
called Combe Florey. As he had Piers Court, Waugh decorated
his new home with Victorian furniture and pictures and souve-
nirs of his travels.

Although he was becoming increasingly ill and difficult,
Waugh was not utterly misanthropic, and the letters and diaries
of the years between 1957 and 1962 indicate that even though
he was not happy he was loving and concerned about his friends
and family. For example, in 1957 his old friend Monsignor Ronald Knox was diagnosed as having cancer. Although the medical
prognosis was entirely hopeless, Knox felt that he might recover

if he could go to the sea. At a time when he felt his own creative sands running out, Waugh took time to accompany Monsignor Knox, first to Torquay and later to Sidmouth, to resort hotels that were not at all what he would have chosen himself. Then he took his old friend home to Combe Florey. It was a loving and selfless action.

In August of 1957, Knox died and *The Ordeal of Gilbert Pinfold* was published. Although Waugh felt and feared that he had only one or two good books left in him, he devoted much time during the next two years to researching and writing a biography of Knox. In the course of doing so, he traveled to Africa, partially to complete his research on Knox, who had close friends there, and partially to seek the sun as he often needed to do during an English winter. The biography of Knox appeared in 1959, and the articles Waugh wrote for the *Sunday Times*, which financed the trip, formed the basis for his last travel book, *A Tourist in Africa*, published in 1960.

As he was completing the details of publication for *Ronald Knox* and *A Tourist in Africa*, Waugh was also beginning work on his last novel, *Unconditional Surrender*, published in the United States as *The End of the Battle*. His son, Auberon, who had been severely wounded while on duty with the armed forces, had recovered enough to enter Oxford University, his daughter Teresa was about to graduate from that institution, and both Auberon and Teresa were about to be married. This must have been another busy and stressful time for Waugh, whose last several books had not been best-sellers, but he still found time to devote to a project that was largely based on love.

From his earliest years, Waugh had been an admirer of the English comic writer, P. G. Wodehouse. He loved Wodehouse's comic inventiveness, the seamlessness of the world he had invented and the characters with whom he had peopled that world. Thus he had long been troubled by the persistence of a story that Wodehouse had been pro-Nazi and had made broadcasts from Germany during World War II that were intended to

give aid and comfort to the enemy. Although most authorities
agreed by 1960 that Wodehouse was more naïve than Nazi, many
people continued to believe that he was a traitor. Waugh found
this state of affairs deplorable and wanted to defend Wodehouse's honor. To do so, he invited himself to speak on the
BBC.

To invite oneself to speak on national radio is probably not
very easy in most circumstances; in Waugh's it was especially
difficult because he had a history of crossing swords with BBC
interviewers, many of whom were young liberals who wanted to
show up the old conservative for the fool he must be. Unfortunately for them, Waugh was no buffoon, and he almost always
left his interviewer looking foolish. This was good for his ego,
but it left him with a distaste for the BBC and its employees.
They felt much the same in return. In any case, Waugh went to
great lengths to work with people he did not particularly care
for in order to try to correct the public perception of Wodehouse's loyalty. Whether he was successful, one cannot know,
but the fact that he made such a broadcast for this cause is
moving.

By 1961, Waugh was an old man, much older than his peers.
His health was bad. He felt his creative powers failing; he saw
his friends dying and watched his circle growing smaller. He
also saw his church, which he always referred to as "the Church,"
undergoing changes that compromised his notions of what Catholicism stood for and offended his sense of literary style. He
wrote little, for him, after *Unconditional Surrender*—a few long short
stories (including *Basil Seal Rides Again*) and the first volume of a
projected three volume autobiography, *A Little Learning*. He re-
vised the war trilogy and issued a recension under the title *Sword
of Honour*. But he was not well and he was not happy. His daughter Margaret later recalled,

After I married, he used to write, not so often, but regularly.
They were sad letters because by this time he was a sad man. What

he saw as the collapse of the Catholic Church, and the loss of his teeth between them robbed him both of his spiritual and physical well being and sapped his already very weak will to live. His faith became a struggle and he gave up eating.[39]

Her analysis certainly seems to fit with the tenor of Waugh's last letters to his friends. He wrote to Nancy Mitford that 1965 "has been a year of deaths"[40] and to Diana Mosely that "Pope John and his Council. . . destroyed the beauty of the liturgy."[41] Perhaps most touching, he quoted Father Hubert van Zeller, saying, "Dying is just growing up. I am not unhappy. I just do not much like being alive."[42]

2

Innocents at Home

For many years, the standard assessment of Waugh's work ran something like this: He began his career as a writer of wide-ranging satire and was justly celebrated for his lacerating wit. His conversion to Catholicism and the advent of his "serious" concerns marked the beginning of a decline in his achievement. Finally, with the exception of *The Loved One*, everything he wrote after *A Handful of Dust* was inferior to those first wonderfully anarchic representations of the adventures of the bright young things.[1]

As is the case with most commonly held opinions, there is some truth in this version of Waugh's development. There is an effortless manic quality to the humor of the early novels (especially *Decline and Fall* and *Vile Bodies*) that is unmatched in the later works, largely because the early novels rely almost exclusively on negative instruction (i.e., ridiculing those things of which one disapproves) to achieve their satiric purposes. The satire is wide-ranging because the fictional world Waugh represents is entirely mad: it is not just mad in certain places, as is the case in the later work. And yet, it does not seem accurate to say that Waugh's career falls neatly into two parts, nor does it seem sensible to claim that the achievement of the early years is superior to that of the latter.

Still, it is easy to understand why six decades of readers have been spellbound by those first volleys fired over the heads of "the older generation," as Waugh was wont to call everyone who was his senior. *Decline and Fall*, *Vile Bodies*, and *Black Mischief* have a boundless energy about them, a powerful sense of forward motion that makes it hard to stop reading once one has started. They evince a wit that seems to look unblinkingly at the idiocies of the real world, and to look with a perfectly straight face at the fantastic improbabilities the author himself creates. And Waugh's bright, sharp style expresses both the energy and the wit faithfully.

In order to argue that the early novels are superior to the later, however, one must argue that a humorous intent is superior to a serious one, and therefore that a novel that is consistently funny is superior to one in which humor is used intermittently to develop a serious theme. To make such an argument may also be to argue that negative instruction (pointing out what is wrong) is superior to positive instruction (pointing out what is right). But in fact, although negative instruction may be easier and may even be funnier, it is not necessarily aesthetically superior. The superior tool is the one that fits the task, and as Waugh's notion of his task changed, his choice of tools changed, too. Further, the choices he made, in both the early and the late stages of his career, were appropriate and effective. Finally, Waugh's work is marked by strong continuities; among those continuities are certain themes (the decline of the modern age, the role of religion in the life of humanity, the function of language, and the essential nature of man as exile) and certain images (circles, buildings, water) as well as an enduring concern with problems of structure and style.

In his earliest novels, Waugh was a farceur of the highest order. Farce is a form of comedy (usually theatrical) populated by characters who are types rather than individuals. It features outrageous and violent actions such as chase scenes, slapstick, practical jokes and the accompanying pratfalls, and it generally insults, or at least attacks, as many of the household gods of family piety and social propriety as fall within its range. Eric Bentley, in his essay "The Psychology of Farce," observes that farce reminds us "that God lavished stupidity on the human race with a recklessly prodigal hand" and that the farceur "must have the gift of some lunatics (such as paranoiacs) to build a large, intricate, and self-consistent structure of improbabilities."[2] Among Waugh's early targets were the major social institutions (religion, education, government, and family) and any one of their authorities.

Decline and Fall

Decline and Fall, Waugh's first novel, is for those who love farce, one of the funniest of English novels. The constant appearance, disappearance, and reappearance in another identity of the characters puts one immediately in mind of the opening and closing doors and the circular structures of plot that characterize farce. Although Waugh's approach is often oblique and ironic rather than straightforward and broadly humorous, it is stunningly effective. Even now, more than fifty years after its original publication, *Decline and Fall* is readily available in bookstores and libraries, and each succeeding generation learns to laugh at the Candide-like existence of Paul Pennyfeather.

Although Waugh had hoped *Decline and Fall* would be a real money maker, it was not. It was, however, very well received by the reviewers, and it brought his name before a much larger audience than his biographical study, *Rossetti*, could ever have done. The *Observer* found it "richly and roaringly funny,"[3] and J. B. Priestley noted that "Mr. Waugh has done something very difficult to do, he has created a really comic character."[4]

The title of the novel cannot but remind the reader of the other great *Decline and Fall*, Gibbon's history of the Roman Empire. In alluding to Gibbon, Waugh suggests to the reader that his book, too, will trace the crimes, follies, and misfortunes of mankind. A second choice for the title, which would have struck the same note but which would have been a little less accessible to the general reader was "Untoward Incidents." Waugh suggested the title to his editor at Duckworth's (where the novel was eventually rejected) and explained, "The phrase, you remember, was used by the Duke of Wellington in commenting on the destruction of the Turkish Fleet in time of peace at Navarino. It seems to set the right tone of mildly censorious detachment."[5] As a description of the authorial tone of *Decline and Fall,* "censorious detachment" is hard to beat.

As the novel opens, Paul Pennyfeather is a student in Scone College of Oxford University and is innocently unaware of the chaotic forces underlying modern society. When he runs the length of the quad in his underwear after his trousers are forcibly removed by the drunken members of the Bollinger Club, Paul is dismissed from his college for "indecent behavior." He leaves Oxford with the words of the college porter in his ears: "I expect you'll be becoming a schoolmaster, sir. That's what most of the gentlemen does, sir, that gets sent down for indecent behavior." Turned out of the house by his greedy guardian who sees a chance to appropriate Paul's inheritance for his own daughter, Paul indeed becomes a schoolmaster at Llanabba Castle, a minor public school in Wales. His fellow masters are Grimes, a pederast who, ironically, comes to represent the forces of life in the novel, and Prendergast, the representative of organized religion, who, again ironically, becomes a symbol of death.

Paul's favorite student at Llanabba is Peter Beste-Chetwynde whose mother, Margot, is an international white slaver. Paul falls in love with Margot and is about to be married to her when she sends him to France to help clear the way for her latest group of South American-bound prostitutes. He succeeds and returns to London only to be arrested on the way to the altar through the efforts of his college chum, Potts (now in the employ of the League of Nations). Convicted of procuring, Paul is sentenced to prison. Margot arranges to have him removed from the prison to a private hospital, ostensibly for an appendectomy. When the proprietor reports to the authorities that he has died on the operating table, Paul escapes to Margot's retreat on Corfu to consider his future. Eventually, he returns to Scone, sporting a new mustache as a disguise and posing as his own cousin.

One of the great appeals of Waugh's fiction is likewise one of the great appeals of those adolescent adventure stories that were the backbone of the nineteenth-century boy's books—the hero is almost always a young man on his own. In Waugh's vision in the early novels, however, the hero has had independence thrust upon him; that is, he is an exile from a society of which he would love to be a part. This is especially true in the first two novels, *Decline and Fall* and *Vile Bodies*.

Paul Pennyfeather, for example, is an orphan. His parents died when he was at public school. His guardian, who has control of Paul's money until Paul is twenty-one, has no compunctions about confiscating the money and throwing Paul out. His teachers are similarly exploitative, more interested in the founder's port than in justice. His employer, Dr. Fagan, and his fiance, Margot, are equally predatory.

Paul's essential feature is his *outsideness* or his status as an exile. Indeed, exile is one of the few consistent aspects of his life. His parents, the narrator reveals, "had died in India at the time when he won the essay prize at his preparatory school." Having survived the first exile (public school) of the English gentleman, Paul is, in short order, exiled from his college and from his home, the house of the prosperous solicitor in Onslow Square. As the novel progresses, Paul finds himself even further estranged from the world he *thought* he knew and the code he *thought* it followed: "For generations the British bourgeoisie have spoken of themselves as gentlemen, and by that they have meant, among other things, a self-respecting scorn of irregular perquisites," he reminds himself. This code, which may work for the British bourgeoisie who can remain safely within the social framework they understand, is woefully inadequate in the chaotic modern world in which the very walls and towers of the old order are being taken down and replaced by vast constructs of chromium and glass. Paul's code, the code of the gentleman, is perfectly admirable, and his ingenuous character is a reflection of that charming construct, but the code cannot, and does not, prepare him to meet the new world that has evolved around him.

Note, for example, that in his first interview with Dr. Fagan, Paul resolves to tell the truth about his past: "I was sent down, sir, for indecent behavior." Dr. Fagan's response, "I have been in the scholastic profession long enough to know that nobody enters it unless he has some very good reason which he is anxious to conceal," simply and wittily illustrates that the world outside Scone College is playing a different game by a set of rules that Paul has not yet even begun to understand.

Similarly, Paul's failure to understand the nature of Margot's business, Latin-American Entertainments, Ltd., and his innocent observation that the League of Nations "seem to make it harder to get about instead of easier," suggest his inability to understand the world or to understand that anyone of his class could be less than honorable. Introducing the first of a long line of doubles in his fiction, Waugh has the narrator observe that Paul Pennyfeather has mysteriously disappeared and will be replaced by a shadow whose only interest "arises from the unusual series of events of which his shadow was witness." In doing so, he suggests that there is something in the air of England at the time that is eliminating the British gentleman and replacing him with an empty facade.

Back in his familiar habitat with Potts, Paul becomes again what he had once been: . . . an intelligent, well-educated, well-conducted young man, a man who could be trusted to use his vote at a general election with discretion and proper detachment, whose opinion on a *ballet* or a critical essay was rather better than most people's, who could order dinner without embarrassment and in a creditable French accent, who could be trusted to see to luggage at foreign railway stations, and might be expected to acquit himself with decision and decorum in all the emergencies of civilized life.

The difficulty, of course, is that the life Waugh surveys in *Decline and Fall* is not what one would call civilized. Thus, as soon as Paul leaves the restaurant and the discussion of Otto Silenus and re-enters the modern world as it is reflected in the new King's Thursday, the man he was educated to be disappears and the shadow he has become appears in his stead.

Paul Pennyfeather is a fine young man with no vices when he is at Scone studying for the church. Despite his virtue, Paul is not very well treated by the authorities at his college. The moral failure of the faculty and administration is clear in the master's deciding to dismiss Paul from the college because he would probably not be able to pay a heavy fine. The Junior Dean and the Domestic Bursar are interested only in the amount of money collected in fines and what that implies for the quality of the after-dinner port. Even the chaplain, who might be expected to demonstrate more charity than the others, fails to acknowledge that Paul has been treated unfairly and that his life has been ruined. The chaplain's concern is solely for himself and for the return of a book he had lent Paul: "Oh, Pennyfeather, before you go, surely you have my copy of Dean Stanley's *Eastern Church?*

Having left Scone, Paul has a series of experiences that are equally hard on the church and churchmen. He first meets Mr. Prendergast, a defrocked clergyman who "lost his faith" because he could not understand, metaphorically, the first thing about his own religion: "You see, it wasn't the ordinary sort of Doubt about Cain's wife or the Old Testament miracles or the consecration of Archbishop Parker. I'd been taught how to explain all that while I was at college. No, it was something deeper than all that. *I couldn't understand why God had made the world at all.*"

Prendy, the reader learns, resigned his ministry for the same reason Paul decided to refuse Digby-Vaine-Trumpington's twenty pounds—it seemed the only honorable thing to do. That certainly sounds like a positive value. The sad condition of religion in the modern world, however, is revealed when Prendy discovers the "Modern Churchman," defined as "a species of person . . . who draws the full salary of a beneficed clergyman and need not commit himself to any religious belief." For strong religious feeling, the only representative in *Decline and Fall* is the lunatic murderer of Prendergast, who has visions of a wonderfully bloody apocalypse and who regards himself as the "sword of Israel" and "the Lion of the Lord's Elect."

Finally, when Paul returns to Scone to read once more for the church, his education seems to focus not on doctrinal development but on heresies: "There was a bishop in Bithynia, Paul learned, who had denied the Divinity of Christ, the immortality of the soul, the existence of good, the legality of marriage and the validity of the Sacrament of Extreme Unction. How right they had been to condemn him." And in the "Epilogue," "So the ascetic Ebionites used to turn towards Jerusalem when they prayed. . . . Quite right to suppress them." Only at a remove of several centuries is it possible for Paul (or modern man, whom he represents) to be certain of anything.

Not only are the public institutions of education and religion ineffectual against the disintegration of modern society, the family as an institution seems helpless as well. Paul's guardian cheats Paul out of his inheritance; Lady Circumference regards her son as "a dunderhead" who "wants beatin' and hittin' and knockin' about generally, and then he'll be no good." Indeed, the very names of Lady Circumference and Lord Tangent suggest that the connection between them is slight at best. The Llanabba bandmaster pimps for his sister-in-law; Grimes regards marriage simply as a hole card to be played only when he is in more trouble than he can manage; and Margot's ill-developed sense of family is so slight as to allow her to demolish the family seat, King's Thursday, and to feel that the primary importance of the family title is that "it may be nice for Peter to have [it] when he grows up."

One can continue to enumerate institutions that fail in *Decline and Fall*. Medicine does not save Tangent, whose heel was merely "grazed" by Prendergast's bullet. At the end of the novel, Paul is taken to Fagan's sanatorium not be cured but to have his death faked so that he can escape from prison. Similarly, the criminal-justice system, which regards Paul as the corrupter of Margot and is itself presented as corrupt (in the behavior of the prison guards) and lunatic (in the behavior of the warden) clearly provides no protection for the innocent abroad in the land.

If every social organization—educational, religious, political—is so obviously unable to hold off the forces of chaos in the novel, how, then, does Waugh manage to bring Paul Pennyfeather to a happy ending of sorts? It is here that the circular structure of the novel, which brings Paul back to the position he occupied at the beginning, and the central powerful symbol of the wheel at Luna Park are particularly helpful.

In the "Prelude" of the novel, Paul Pennyfeather is in "his third year of uneventful residence at Scone"; that is, he is nearly at the end of his conventional education. He has spent the evening at a meeting of "the League of Nations Union" and has heard "a most interesting paper about plebiscites in Poland." His idea of relaxation is to read a little of the *Forsyte Saga*, an Edwardian rendition of the instinct to possess and the shattering of social values following World War I. He knows nothing of the behavior or even of the existence of the Bollinger Club, a group representing all that is degenerate, ignorant, prejudiced, and destructive.

The "Epilogue" recapitulates the "Prelude." From the opening sentence, "It was Paul's third year of uneventful residence at Scone" and Stubbs' observation, "That was an interesting paper tonight about the Polish plebiscites," there is every indication that Waugh intends the reader to hear what he has heard before. But I think we must differ with James F. Carens's assessment that "[Paul] dies, he reappears, but he is not reborn. Nothing that has happened has had any effect upon him,"[6] for Paul's responses are vastly different the second time around. This time, he is finishing his real education.

The second time around, Paul knows about the Bollinger Club and has sense enough not to attract their attention. In his dialogue with Peter Pastmaster, Paul's responses to the boy's drunken questions are a series of assertions, "I remember." And it is remembering that helps to keep him safe. Something less prosaic and more threatening, however, has also happened to Paul, and, it seems to be argued, is helping to keep him safe. Paul has replaced the worldly vision of *The Forsyte Saga* with the history of the church. His view of the "ascetic Ebionites [who] used to turn towards Jerusalem when they prayed" is the view of a detached scholar rather than that of a participant in life. It is true that his detachment will protect him from the wasteland of Llanabba Castle and Blackstone Gaol, but it will also separate him from the voluptuous richness and excess of Margot Metroland and those other "dynamic" characters of whom Professor Silenus, that Dionysian spirit, once spoke. The modern world has cast him out just as he would cast out the "ascetic Ebionites" and the notorious Bishop of Bithynia.

Waugh also uses the descriptions of Paul's three celebratory meals to call attention to the circularity of the world he is describing. The first is with Grimes and Prendy at Llanabba Castle; the second is with Alastair Digby-Vaine-Trumpington and Peter Beste-Chetwynde at the Ritz, and the third is with Dr. Fagan and Alastair at Fagan's sanatorium where Paul's death has just been falsely reported. The parallels are instructive.

At the first dinner, which takes place in part one, Paul, Prendy and Grimes celebrate Paul's "recent good fortune" (on the face of it the twenty pounds he has from Alastair Digby-Vaine-Trumpington, but in reality his liberation from the closed existence he has had at Scone College) and Grimes's impending

marriage. The irony is lavish here, since what is depicted is
Paul's first compromise with his image of himself as a gentleman.
His earlier toast, "To the durability of ideals," is a wonderful
illustration of the way Waugh makes meaning change by changing context. When Paul first uses the phrase, "the durability of
ideals," he is really talking with himself about who he is and
about the nature of the English gentleman. He explains at some
length that in refusing Digby-Vaine-Trumpington's money he is
satisfying "a test case of the durability of my ideals." When,
however, Grimes reveals that he has saved Paul from himself by
accepting Trumpington's money for him, Paul feels ". . . a great
wave of satisfaction surge up within him." When he repeats the
toast, "To the durability of ideals," he, like the reader, is conscious of the irony involved.

The meal motif is picked up in the scene depicting Paul's
wedding luncheon at the Ritz, where a new toast is introduced.
"To Fortune—a much maligned lady" is the utterance of a con-
tented man who has once again closed his eyes to all of the
ungentlemanly activities of the world around him. Alastair's ingenuous observation "No one could have guessed that when I
had the Boller blind in my rooms it was going to end like this"
seems to signal a happy ending; in fact, it only signals another
complication as Inspector Bruce of Scotland Yard arrests Paul as
an international white slaver and closes another episode in his
eventful life.

The third celebratory meal takes place in part three after
Paul is freed from prison through a scheme in which he is falsely
declared to have died in a hospital. Dr. Fagan, once the head
of Llanabba school and now the proprietor of a private hospital,
articulates the importance of Paul's "death," by noting that "it is
the beginning of a new phase of life." When Dr. Fagan proposes
the toast "To Fortune—a much maligned lady," he is toasting
the end of Paul's life as a convict and his rebirth as a student of
theology.

The final version of the toast occurs in the closing scene

when Peter Beste-Chetwynde (now Peter Pastmaster) appears in
Paul's rooms in college. In the "Epilogue" as in the "Prelude," the
"annual gathering of the Bollinger" coincides with Paul's "third
year of uneventful residence at Scone." At Scone, as at the Ritz
years earlier, Peter is a little drunk. In fact, he is so drunk that,
having reiterated Paul's toast, "To Fortune—a much maligned
lady," he immediately finds himself unable to recall how it goes.

Paul's values and those of Otto Silenus form an interesting
and informative contrast. Silenus, who in mythology was a forest spirit, the oldest of the satyrs, and the foster father and
teacher of Dionysus, finds an ironic namesake in the young architect whose instincts are fundamentally anti-social (his artistic
credo is "the elimination of the human element from the consideration of form") and whose counsel is to avoid participation in
life and to seek stasis. To make his point, he compares life to a
ride on the great wheel at Luna Park. The great wheel is a ro-
tating disk and the challenge is to stay aboard it once it begins
to spin. Professor Silenus explains,

People don't see that when they say "life" they mean two different
things. They can mean simply existence, with its physiological implications of growth and organic change. They can't escape that—even
by death, but because that's inevitable they think the other side of life
is too—the scrambling and excitement and bumps and the effort to
get to the middle. And when we do get to the middle, it's just as if
we never started.

Paul, on the other hand, is of a type open to much human
experience but with the perspective of the old, the traditional,
the poetic, the nonmechanistic about him. His love for Margot
is born of a response to her physical beauty, a beauty which
seems at first immortal but which he comes to fear is all too
transitory. His imaginative vision of King's Thursday is pure
nineteenth century romanticism:

"English spring," thought Paul. "In the dreaming ancestral beauty of the English country." Surely, he thought, these great chestnuts in the morning sun stood for something enduring and serene in a world that had lost its reason and would so stand when the chaos and confusion were forgotten.

For Otto Silenus, however, Margot's beauty is not poetic at all. For him, "in all her essential functions—her digestion for example—she conforms to type." His strictly mechanistic view is also reflected in his first question to Paul: "What do you take to make you sleep?" Paul, by contrast, takes nothing to make him sleep and rests easily throughout the novel—in Scone College, in King's Thursday, and back in Scone.

Withdrawal from life may be advisable, but it is not a very positive solution to the problem. If this is a world in which people are rewarded strictly according to the laws of chance rather than according to the laws of merit, then there is nothing a person like Paul can do except refuse to live, for he does not seem to be blessed with traditional luck. If, on the other hand, Paul's bad treatment at the hands of the world is appropriate, what has he done to deserve it? His only error is innocence— ignorance of the ways of the world. Seen in that light, the structure of the novel is not comic but ironic, for it is a structure in which a fundamentally blameless fellow is treated much more badly than he deserves. On the other hand, Paul is not real; he has no feelings or motives and, in the way farce works, he isn't damaged by anything that happens to him. He simply comes back, good as new, after his pratfalls.

Thus *Decline and Fall* tells a very funny story with a very discomfiting implication. True to the conventions of farce, characters in *Decline and Fall* disappear through one door to reappear, in a different form, through another. Paul's "great friend," Potts, reappears as the League of Nations representative whose work leads to Paul's arrest and conviction. Dr. Fagan, the headmaster of Llanabba Castle, reappears as the proprietor of the private hospital where Paul "dies" and as the author of a book on Welsh culture called *Mother Wales*. Grimes, the pederastic master at Llanabba, is first transformed into the "manager" of one of Margot's South American enterprises and then into a convict. Prendergast, the other master, becomes a modern churchman; and Philbrick the butler, that master of intrigue and disguise, finally appears in Oxford in an open motor car, looking very like one of the idle rich.

Thematically, the fact that nearly all the characters in *Decline and Fall* play multiple roles is significant. First, it suggests that reality is not very stable in this world, and that one might well be exceptionally careful in making judgments, because things are almost never what they seem to be. In addition, it is significant in determining the ways one can think about the characters in the novel. If Paul Pennyfeather is sometimes a nice young man studying for the ministry, sometimes a social celebrity, and sometimes a convict, how is one to think about him as a real person with real emotions, real motives and believable responses to events? The short answer is that one cannot. One cannot talk sensibly about how this character might reasonably be expected to act because one has no real sense of who he is. He is a type, and the type is the innocent. But he is never flesh and blood.

In *Decline and Fall*, as in his next two novels, Waugh restricted his characters to these comic types in order to avoid engaging his readers' emotions. Instead, he encourages his readers to a distanced, intellectual enjoyment of his indictment of a world where chance reigns supreme, ideals are superfluous if not outright dangerous, and the laws of cause and effect have been suspended.

Vile Bodies

The essential components of farce, at least in popular usage, are a husband, a wife, a lover, and a room with many doors; or, as

Eric Bentley explains, farce deals "with some absurd situation hinging generally on extra-marital relations—hence the term bedroom farce."[7] Among Waugh's farces, *Vile Bodies* comes closest to being a classic bedroom farce.

Vile Bodies was a popular and financial success and confirmed Waugh's place as an important young writer. V. S. Pritchett, writing in the *Spectator*, claimed, "I laughed until I was driven out of the room."[8] And Rebecca West, in an extended commentary in the *Fortnightly Review* asserted that "*Vile Bodies*, has, indeed, apart from its success in being really funny, a very considerable value as a further stage in the contemporary literature of disillusionment."[9] Other critics were, however, less impressed by this second novel. Ralph Straus, although he loved the book, felt that "you cannot be given an outline of the plot, for the simple reason that there is none,"[10] and in the *Evening Standard* Arnold Bennett judged that the novel "has a few satirical sallies of the first order of merit, but the lack of a well-laid plot has resulted in a large number of pages which demand a certain obstinate and sustained effort of will for their perusal."[11]

Waugh himself felt that *Vile Bodies* was inferior to *Decline and Fall*, but it is difficult to be sure whether his dissatisfaction with the work was based strictly on artistic grounds or resulted from his extreme personal unhappiness at the time he was working on it. Whatever the origin of his reservations, he expressed them clearly to his friend Henry Yorke (the novelist Henry Green): "I put off going abroad and came here to make a last effort at finishing my novel. It has been infinitely difficult and is certainly the last time I shall try to make a book about sophisticated people. It all seems to shrivel up & rot internally and I am relying on a sort of cumulative futility for any effect it may have."[12]

Vile Bodies is the story of Adam Fenwick-Symes, a young writer (and another orphan) who, as the novel opens, is engaged to Nina Blount, one of the bright young people and daughter of an eccentric aristocrat. When customs officials seize and burn the manuscript of the autobiography Adam has just completed, he is sent careening through a series of irrational episodes in search of the money that will allow him to marry Nina. Before he succeeds in finding it, Nina marries the thick-headed but moneyed Ginger, and war in Europe, foreshadowed throughout the novel, finally breaks out.

Upon first returning to England from France, Adam goes to Lottie Crump's hotel where one could "draw up, cool and un-contaminated, great healing draughts from the well of Edwar-dian certainty." There he wins a thousand pounds in a parlor game and can marry Nina. He gives the thousand pounds to a drunk major to bet on a horse race (he can't marry Nina). He goes to Nina's very eccentric father for help and is given a check for a thousand pounds (he can marry Nina). He discovers hours later that the check is signed "Charlie Chaplin" (he can't marry Nina). He takes a job as a gossip columnist for a daily newspa-per; he loses the job. He finds the drunk major at a race course; he loses him again; he finds him once more on a foreign battle-field. And throughout, Adam's pursuit of Nina and the thousand pounds is punctuated by the parties of the bright young people whose headlong pursuit of amusement leads to untoward inci-dents ranging from a butler's attack of the DTs to the death of Agatha Runcible, to the fall of several governments.

In Waugh's realization that the primary effect of *Vile Bodies* was "a sort of cumulative futility," and in Rebecca West's obser-vation that the novel was part of the "literature of disillusion-ment," one sees indications that Adam's situation, even more than Paul's, is one of exile; he operates on the fringes of every social set, belonging to none. The difference between the exiles of Paul and Adam is that in the world of *Vile Bodies* it is no longer possible to ameliorate the dangers of exile by choosing to sit still. Like Paul, Adam is completely alone in the world. At the novel's opening, he is in France alone. His mother and father are dead. Although he has become engaged to Nina, there is a lack of engagement between the two of them that suggests an instability in their relationship. They communicate imperfectly by telephone (Nina always has "rather a pain") and not much more completely face to face. The tenuousness of the connection is perhaps best illustrated by the frequency with which the engagement is ended and begun again as Adam's fortunes ebb and flow. His telephone messages, "We can't get married" and "We can get married, after all," are not only a unifying device in the novel, they are also an indication of the chaotic quality of Adam's and Nina's lives.

Adam's home, if he has a home in *Vile Bodies*, is Lottie Crump's hotel. It, too, is chaotic, with its champagne parties, bills that get "rather muddled sometimes," and "sound old snobbery of pounds sterling and strawberry leaves." But even at Lottie's, Adam is on the fringe. The people at Lottie's have no names (Adam is "Lord Thingummy," the others include "Mr. What's-his-name," "Mr. What-d'you-call-him," and the major). Part of the attraction of the hotel is that it is outside the mainstream, and Lottie is at pains to keep it that way. However, Shepherd's has nothing of value to offer as an alternative to the unsatisfactory modern world. Its "Edwardian certainty" is as empty and chaotic as modern uncertainty.

Even when Adam is at his happiest, he is alone. After visiting Nina's father at the appropriately named "Doubting 'All," sitting through a lunch in which no conversation takes place, and spending the afternoon alone in the library, Adam has come back with a check for a thousand pounds. He finds Nina at a party he cannot bear to join ("I couldn't face a party. I'm so excited") and dances alone in the foyer. Nina later observes: "It's awful to think that I shall probably never, as long as I live, see you dancing like that again all by yourself." She is partly right; she may never see him dance for happiness again, but if she does one can bet he will be alone.

Like Paul's fortunes, then, Adam's fortunes rise and fall without rhyme or reason. But to be at the mercy of fortune in *Vile Bodies* is rather more dangerous than it was in *Decline and Fall*. At the close of *Vile Bodies* the modern world has reached its inevitable destination—total war and "the biggest battlefield in the history of the world." All that remains is the transitory physical pleasure symbolized by champagne and sex. The hopelessness of the future is implied by the final scene in which the money Adam has sought is devalued, the world he wanted to enter is replaced by a scene of "unrelieved desolation," and the sounds of battle have begun to return. The desolation is so great that it is almost true to say that Adam is no longer in exile because there is nothing left to be exiled from.

Vile Bodies reveals two characteristics of farce that are helpful in understanding the structure of the novel and its themes: the confusion of appearance and reality is expressed through both the confusion of identities of the characters and the setting aside of the laws of cause and effect. As in *Decline and Fall*, the switching of identities is an important device in the novel, both thematically and stylistically. Thematically, the device develops the confusion of appearance and reality. For example, Mrs. Melrose Ape's angel, Chastity, is anything but an angel and anything but chaste. From the first moment she is introduced, when Mrs. Ape acerbically comments that whenever there is work to be done, Chastity isn't feeling well, through Chastity's adventures with Mrs. Panrast, to the last scene of the novel when she reappears in the back seat of the drunk major's Daimler, Chastity is in and out of more compromising positions than seems possible. She has been hired as a prostitute by Margot Metroland and has serviced the troops of almost every army involved in the war with which the novel ends. Candide-like, however, she always reappears. In doing so, she abundantly illustrates the point that in the world of *Vile Bodies* things are not only not what they seem, they are not even what they seem to seem.

Similarly, Mrs. Panrast, who is at best a shadowy character, illustrates how appearances are not to be trusted. In one of the funniest small scenes, the other angels interrogate Chastity about Mrs. Panrast, for "It's not like you, Chastity, to go riding in a motor car with a woman." The confusion is dispelled hilariously

and at the expense of all parties equally when Chastity con-
fesses, "if you must know, I thought she *was* a man."

Although Mrs. Panrast and Chastity are among the best examples of Waugh's use of the confusion of identity in *Vile Bodies*,
they are by no means the only examples. Consider also the case
of Agatha Runcible who assumes so many and various roles in
the novel that she is finally unable to recognize herself. The
first instance is the costume party where the entire younger set
comes dressed as savages and assumes the false identities that
suggest its members don't know who they are. When the youngest
Miss Brown takes Miss Runcible, dressed as a "Hottentot," home
to her family, the family's determination to behave as if nothing
extraordinary is happening while their language reveals how
nonplussed they are is quite funny. But Miss Brown's family is
not as funny as Miss Runcible, who reads aloud three-quarters
of a newspaper article describing the party of which she was a
part before she realizes that she is the subject. Waugh's simile
here is wonderfully vivid:

Suddenly light came flooding in on Miss Runcible's mind as once when,
in her debutante days, she had gone behind the scenes at a charity
matinee, and returning had stepped through the wrong door and found
herself in a blaze of flood-lights on the stage in the middle of the last
act of Othello. "Oh, my God!" she said.

On the stage, the intrusion of reality into the carefully constructed appearance can be as devastating as the replacement of
reality by appearance in the real world. For Miss Runcible, however, the two are incomprehensibly confused.

The second incident in which Miss Runcible loses track of
her identity is the motor race. Bedecked with an armband that
identifies her as "Spare Driver" and having drunk quantities of
the gin and champagne that are always there when the younger
set appears, Miss Runcible makes the mistake of confusing what
she is with what she is called, and she does so in the most self-

destructive way. Referring to the brassard inscribed "spare driver," given to her to disguise the fact that she has no business being in the pits, the intoxicated Miss Runcible offers to take the place of an injured driver: " 'I'm spare driver,' said Miss Runcible. 'It's on my arm.' " This lapse of linguistic logic comes as close as anything in the novel to being the cause of Agatha Runcible's death.

The most extravagant example of shifting identity, however, is the character of Adam Fenwick-Symes, and his foil is Nina's father, Colonel Blount. Adam's first identity is that of a young and reportedly talented writer. From that happy state he is transformed into Mr. Chatterbox, the gossip columnist, replacing the unfortunate Simon Balcairn who kills himself after reporting in fascinating and libelous detail an imaginary account of a party from which he was ejected. The irony is that none of the real gossip Simon reported was half as interesting as the imaginary gossip Adam produces in its place.

After losing his place as Mr. Chatterbox in turn, Adam is once more transformed, this time into his own rival for Nina's hand, Ginger Littlejohn. As Captain Littlejohn, he accompanies Nina to her father's house for the Christmas holidays just as he would have done had he been the successful suitor.

Finally, Adam is transformed into a war hero, and the transformation is accomplished exactly as all the others have been: saying it makes it so. He learns of his status in a letter from Nina, who writes, "Van has got a divine job making up all the war news, and he invented a lovely story about you the other day, how you'd saved hundreds of people's lives, and there's what they call a popular agitation saying why haven't you got the V.C., so probably you will have by now. Isn't it amusing?"

The second characteristic of farce that has important thematic meaning in *Vile Bodies* is the inappropriateness of cause to effect. For example, when Mr. Brown's government falls because of the treatment of Agatha Runcible by the customs inspectors, the effect seems absurdly out of proportion to the cause. Simi-

"I said, I see."
"Is that all?"
"Yes, that's all, Adam."
"I'm sorry."
"I'm sorry, too. Good-bye."

This is not quite all, but it does demonstrate what Rebecca West was getting at when she wrote of Waugh's style in *Vile Bodies*, "In the monosyllabic conversations of [Adam and Nina], brief as canary cheep, Mr. Waugh has done something as technically astonishing as the dialogues in Mr. Ernest Hemingway's *Farewell to Arms*, so cunningly does he persuade the barest formula to carry a weight of emotion."[13]

The point of view adopted to present the vignettes of which the novel is composed is third person limited. The limitation is appropriate, of course, because the inability of the participants to make the connections is part of the theme of the novel. The only stylistic false step Waugh makes is to drop occasionally into an attitude of omniscience. Now and then, the narrator wants to step into the work and address the reader directly, usually to point out the folly of his characters' behavior. For example, when Adam and Nina quarrel after having spent their first night together, the narrator observes: "The truth is that like so many people of their age and class, Adam and Nina were suffering from being sophisticated about sex before they were at all widely experienced." These narrative intrusions are not consistent with the tone of the rest of the work, so they constitute a flaw, although not a grave one.

Vile Bodies is far more elegiac in tone than *Decline and Fall*. In *Vile Bodies* Waugh begins to long for the past and to fear the future in a way that occurs rarely if at all in the earlier novel. In Nina's observation that she will never again see Adam dancing all alone for pure joy, for example, there is an echo of "The Last Tournament" of Tennyson's *Idylls of the King* that is quite touching. Similarly, the evocation of Lottie Crump's hotel is a celebration of the past: "One can go to Shepheard's parched with modernity any day, if Lottie likes one's face, and still draw up, cool and uncontaminated, great, healing draughts from the well of Edwardian certainty."

Father Rothschild, who possesses above anyone else in the novel an intelligent and consistent point of view, observes that the bright young people are victims of "an almost fatal hunger for permanence," which they feel ended with the last war. (In this way, they are like the last generations of *The Forsyte Saga*.) Father Rothschild continues to evoke their sense of loss, saying,

People aren't content just to muddle along nowadays. My private schoolmaster used to say, 'If a thing's worth doing at all, it's worth doing well.' My church has taught that in different words for several centuries. But these young people have got hold of another end of the stick, and for all we know it may be the right one. They say, 'If a thing's not worth doing well, it's not worth doing at all.' It makes everything very difficult for them.

The central notion of the novel is, to use Father Rothschild's phrasing, that "there is a radical instability in our whole world-order" that will ultimately result in destruction. This radical instability refers not just to the political arena, but to all areas of human life, including language.

Black Mischief

With *Black Mischief* (1932) Waugh began to adopt the practice of using materials developed in his travel books (here *Labels* and *Remote People*) as the basis for incidents in his fiction. Also, for the first time, he was reviewed, and not terribly favorably, as a Catholic writer. In fact, most reviewers found the novel to be a qualified success. The *Daily Telegraph* detected "an air of uncertainty . . . which we did not find in his previous novels",[14] the *Daily Express* found the satire "heavy-handed,"[15] and *Bookman* lamented that "Mr. Waugh still seems to suffer from his early illusion that the vapid fatuities of Ronald Firbank are funny."[16] Where most reviewers found a good, though flawed, performance, however, the Catholic *Tablet* found anathema. Ernest Oldmeadow, the *Tablet's* editor took the position that *Black Mischief* "would be a disgrace to anyone professing the Catholic name"[17] and in two subsequent numbers of the publication spent several thousands of words justifying his position and questioning Waugh's commitment to his newly adopted religion.

What seems to have set Oldmeadow off first was an episode of cannibalism that, stated baldly, certainly doesn't sound amusing. In the context of this satirical novel, however, it is more than moderately funny. *Black Mischief* is the story of two young Oxford undergraduates, Seth and Basil Seal. The first half of the novel is dominated by Seth, the young emperor of Azania, an island empire in the Indian Ocean, who is caught up in a revolution that takes place in his twenty-fourth year. In an attempt to modernize a country where defeated leaders are eaten and wars are won by two ancient weapons, lies and the long spear, Seth appoints the lazy and manipulative, but clearly modern Basil as his Minister of Modernization. When Seth's government is finally overthrown, Basil's girlfriend is captured by a native tribe whose leaders serve her up in a ceremonial stew at Seth's burial celebration. It was Basil's participation in those ceremonies and his partaking of that stew that so distressed Mr. Oldmeadow. He seems not to have appreciated the delicious irony of having the Minister of Modernization participate in a clearly ancient and uncivilized tradition.

In *Black Mischief*, one feels for the first time that Waugh's satire has a definite purpose to it, that instead of simply observing the foibles of modern mankind and enjoying the lunacy for its own sake, he has identified some qualities he genuinely deplores. Among these are the mindless pursuit of progress, the cosmic stupidity of officers of government, and the credulity and excesses excited by formal religion.

The novel is divided into two parts. In the first part the reader meets three groups of characters—the Azanian court, the British diplomatic staff, and the English friends of Basil Seal. The young emperor, Seth, has been called home from Oxford to assume the throne upon the death of his mother. As the book opens, he is engaged in a civil war with the forces of his father, Seyid, and is justifiably feeling deserted by all his associates except General Connolly, the Scottish commander in chief of the Azanian armed forces.

General Connolly's victory over the insurgents is a great relief to members of the British diplomatic staff who are leading a completely English style of life a few miles outside the capital city of Debra-Dowa. Although they are almost oblivious to the events around them, the envoy, his wife, his daughter Prudence, and the other residents of the compound are greatly relieved when the fighting stops and the "bag" from England with its new records, magazines, and letters from home arrives. This happily unconscious crew is under the constant observation of the French diplomatic service, which sees in its activities evidence of an English conspiracy with Seth to take over the country. As a result, the French back and sometimes even incite resistance to the young emperor.

Into this lunatic environment plunges Basil Seal, one of the most talented and amoral of Waugh's bright young people. Unable to generate the steady application and hard work required for success in England, Basil resolves to go to Azania where history is happening. In Debra-Dowa, Seth sees Basil and resolves that this model of modern manhood shall be his Minister of Modernization, charged to "promote the adoption of modern organisation and habits of life throughout the Azanian Empire."

In the second half of the novel, Basil attempts to modernize the empire as Seth's schemes for doing so come faster and in more fragmented forms. A birth-control pageant is organized, and an urban-renewal project is begun, which requires demolishing the Anglican Cathedral and building a European-style city with roads leading out from the center like the spokes of a wheel (this in a country where the road from the capital to the British embassy has been impassable by car for years). There is a plan for a natural history museum and an institute for astronomical research. And it's all financed by the Royal Band of Azania—assets nothing.

While Seth dreams and Basil schemes, the French opposition discovers a rightful heir to the throne in the person of Achon, Seth's uncle. Achon was reported eaten by a lion as a child but has actually been held captive in the Nestorian monastery of St. Mark the Evangelist. When civil war breaks out again, Seth is killed, Achon dies of exhaustion at his own coronation, and the British legation is evacuated (in the process, the airplane in which Prudence is traveling goes down in the bush). Basil, Minister of Modernization, is left to escort the body of the emperor Seth to his tribe for a funeral. Amidst dancing and self-mutilation, the chiefs, including Basil, sit down to a ceremonial dinner. The main dish is a stew that Basil finally discovers is based on Prudence.

When one says that *Black Mischief* falls into two pieces, one speaks not only of the architecture of the novel but of the treatment of the hero. In the first half of the book, Seth and his perceptions are undoubtedly the focus of interest. In the second half, however, Basil Seal takes over, and Seth's creation of problems for Basil is much more interesting than Seth's own problems. It is almost as if Seth and Basil are two competitors for the role of hero, and the minute Basil comes on the scene, Seth begins to disappear.

As in *Decline and Fall* and *Vile Bodies*, the hero of *Black Mischief* is an orphan and an exile. For Seth, the situation of being alone in the world is made a little more dramatic than for Paul or Adam, for Seth has to be responsible for the death of his own

father, Seyid, eaten by the Wanda at the end of the first civil
war. Indeed, much is made of Seth's being "alone" throughout
the novel—from the moment the treacherous secretary, Ali, sees
it as an advantage to the time Dame Mildred and Miss Tin see
"a young man working alone . . . battering at the granite arch-
way at the West End with an energy very rare among Azanian
navvies."

Seth's loneliness and isolation are functions of psychological
and physical realities. Much of his sense of exile comes from his
inability to make his adopted code of European modernism fit
his circumstances. In this he resembles Paul Pennyfeather. At
times the disjunction can seem to reflect modern society's superiority to the ignorance of a traditional culture, as when the
Azanians interpret Seth's birth control posters to mean that large
families are best, even though they may result in poverty and
illness:

See: on right hand: there is rich man: smoke pipe like big chief:
but his wife she no good: sit eating meat: and rich man no good: he
only one son.
See: on left hand: poor man: not much to eat: but his wife she
very good, work hard in field: man he good, too: eleven children: one
very mad, very holy. And in middle: Emperor's juju. Make you like
that good man with eleven children.

Thus the Azanians hurry to buy condoms in order to increase
the size of their families.

As often as the European culture tries to assert its superiority over the Azanian, however, Azanian geography and culture
triumph over the Europeans. For example, there is the matter
of Connolly and the tank. While it is true that the tank is superior in technology to the long spear, it is also true that the
tank is unusable in the Azanian environment: "My dear boy,"
says Connolly, "you can't take a machine like that over this
country under this sun. The whole thing was red hot after five

miles." From the reader's perspective, then, a part of Seth's isolation comes from his inability to respond appropriately to his surroundings. He is alienated psychologically and physically from his environment, and his inappropriate responses to it become a long-running joke that consistently caps itself.

Seth is more clearly and more completely isolated than either Paul or Adam. Where they are both orphans, Seth is saddled with a father who leads a rebellion against him. Even the sense of continuity in the line of Amurath is undercut by the reader's awareness that Amurath came out of the sea from an unknown heritage and that with the deaths of Achon and Seth the line ends.

In addition to Seth, one must consider his double, Basil, in thinking about the importance of exile in *Black Mischief.* Seth's inability to function as a part of the modern world is clear and demonstrable. Even in death, Seth is emphatically separated from the world of which he aspires to be a part. For all his efforts to bring Azania into the twentieth century, his funeral is celebrated in the old way. Basil's eulogy evokes Seth as a great and terrible warrior, whereas he wanted to be known as a master of civilized governance; and as a virile and prolific husband, lover, and father, whereas he wanted to be a champion of birth control. Seth's continuing concern with introducing modern dietary practices among his savage countrymen is capped for the last time when his funeral feast is revealed to be a stew based on Prudence. Death is the ultimate form of exile, and cannibalism is the ultimate repudiation of Seth's aspirations.

One sees in Seth's Azania, of course, a reflection of the modern world as Waugh saw it. The chicanery, both petty and grand, of the Azanian infighters is no greater than that of the British who are sent to Azania by the League of Nations. And the cannibalism of the Wanda vividly symbolizes the destruction that the world can work on those who, like Prudence, play at being engaged.

As the man who survives in the modern world, *Black Mischief* offers Basil Seal. Unlike his ingenuous fellows, Basil is of a temperament that matches, if it does not exceed, the chaotic world of the 1930s. The unprincipled Mr. Youkoumian may prosper by pursuing his creed, "I don't want no bust-ups," but Basil does want them. There is nothing he enjoys so much as a good scene, whether it involves being drunk and disorderly at the Conservative Ball, crashing a party at Margot Metroland's and lecturing her guests on current topics, stealing from his mother, seeking a confrontation with General Connolly, or terrorizing the British Legation with tales of Sakuyu savagery. He lacks loyalty, the ability to commit, in every instance. He is completely self-centered despite the attempts of those about him (his sister, his mother, his lover, and Seth) to pull him into their spheres. Basil, then, is also an outsider; but he is an outsider who is not trying to get in. His isolation is not the isolation of the exile, but the isolation of the uncommitted, the ego-centered, the immature.

One sees in Seth, in broadly comic form, the first outlines of Waugh's next major character, Tony Last—a modern man who has fallen into the hands of savages—and as Tony finds in *A Handful of Dust*, the savages may be at home or abroad. It is difficult, for example, to persuade oneself that the savagery of the Earl of Ngumo or Viscount Boaz is greater than that of Ali, the Indian secretary who betrays Seth in the early scenes. And it is equally difficult to say that Ali's betrayal of Seth is more barbarous than Mr. Youkoumian's treatment of his wife. Further, it is difficult to demonstrate that Mr. Youkoumian's behavior differs substantially from that of Sir Samson who would rather leave Dame Mildred and Miss Tin to the rioters in Debra-Dowa than have them in his compound. And Sir Samson's attitude is certainly no more reprehensible than that of his secretaries who have the following conversation:

"Well, the old girls don't seem to be here. These chaps say they haven't seen anyone."

   And another answered: "I daresay they've been raped."
   "I hope so. Let's try the Mission."

It is, in short, a whole world of savages in different kinds of
dress.
   Waugh's choice of setting in *Black Mischief* reinforces the
notion of isolation that informs the novel. Like the island kingdom, each of the characters is cut off from the world around
him. As the characters are so simplified, it cannot be sensible to
talk about their isolation in terms of character or personality,
but through them Waugh depicts, not the occasional isolation
of individuals or even types, but the necessary isolation, even in
society, of modern man. And all this, of course, in a novel that
was clearly, as he said of another of his books, "intended to be
funny."
   Not only is the island nation, like Britain, cut off from the
neighboring land mass, but within that island various people are
cut off. Sir Samson's great defeat in Azania, for example, is his
failure to have a road built that would connect the British compound to the capital city. As a consequence, the representatives
of the British government in Azania can be as unresponsive to
British subjects as the government in England can. The dream
of Amurath, a railway system that sounds very like the British
system with its "elaborate time-table of express trains, local trains,
goods trains, boat trains, schemes for cheap return tickets and
excursions" consistently fails to provide the connections among
people Waugh seems to be seeking. By the end of the novel, a
bridge has washed out and there is no connection between the
interior and Matodi. And as Prudence's fate illustrates, not even
the modern technology of the airplane can ensure the connections.
   As in his earlier books, Waugh limits his characters severely
for his comic purposes: it would be very nearly impossible, one
would think, to be funny about political betrayal, intrigue, mur-

der, and cannibalism if any of the characters involved were realistic. However, Seth, Connolly, Basil, Prudence, et al are really only flat characters, indeed almost caricatures, so the events that effect them touch the reader almost not at all. One is simply amused by the ironic appropriateness of the events or by the other characters' offhand acceptance of them. For example, at one point Basil says, as he seduces her, "You're a grand girl, Prudence, and I'd like to eat you." Then, at Seth's funeral, he does. A more conscious but equally understated response comes to the death of Seth's father, who is eaten by his enemies. Seth says, "They should not have eaten him—after all he was my father. . . .It is so. . . so barbarous." Connolly immediately agrees: "I knew you'd feel that way about it Seth, and I'm sorry. I gave the headmen twelve hours in the tank for it."

The source of the humor in the case of Seth is his monomania. He has but one theme and that is modernization. Its first clear statement is in Seth's exhortation to his Indian secretary:

This is not a war of Seth against Seyid but of Progress against Barbarism. And Progress must prevail. I have seen the great tattoo of Aldershot, the Paris Exhibition, the Oxford Union. I have read modern books—Shaw, Arlen, Priestley. . . . The whole might of Evolution rides behind [Seyid]: at my stirrups run women's suffrage, vaccination, and vivisection. I am the New Age, I am the future.

What he really is, unfortunately, is an undigested mixture of discrete facts, objects, and ideas. Note, too, how Waugh ridicules Seth by using the principle of anticlimax in his speech—that Seth cannot separate the important aspects of the modern age from the trivial is an indictment of both Seth and the time.

The humor in Waugh's presentation of Seth stems from the repetition of "progress" and "modern" in his speech and from the repetition of Mr. Youkoumian's response to Seth's ideas: "You won't get no peace from im not till you fix im with a woman." As the novel progresses, Seth's reiteration of the ideas of progress and the modern age come faster and faster until, suddenly, he disappears altogether.

If Seth alone had to carry the burden of Waugh's disgust with the mindless pursuit of progress, there might be some justice in considering *Black Mischief* to be a racist book. However, Waugh is at some pains to draw parallels among his three societies, with the result that Seth's foibles find echoes elsewhere in the novel. For example, early in the novel Seth decrees that raw beef is no longer to be served at state dinners—it is not modern. That is, he foolishly proposes to change peoples' eating habits by royal decree. Similarly, at Margot Metroland's party, Lord Monomark lectures the guests on the virtues of luncheons consisting of "two raw onions and a plate of oatmeal porridge. . . .If I had my way . . . I'd make it compulsory throughout the country." That is, like Seth, he would pass a law. The final twist on this continuing joke comes when Basil is charged with implementing the change for Seth. He cuts the Gordian knot by deciding to replace the forbidden raw beef with steak tartare—something quite in accordance with modern thought. Like many of Waugh's best jibes, this one cuts both ways.

Similarly, the theme of corruption and incompetence among the bureaucracy cuts across national lines. In the opening pages of the novel, Seth's officers betray him, one after the other. Marx is said to have stolen the emperor's motorboat and to have charged the gasoline to the imperial account. Ali tries to betray his emperor and does betray Mr. Youkoumian; when he tries to compromise Major Joab, he is strangled for his pains. All this suggests a game in which all the players are corrupt. The European influence, however, seems to make little difference. When Basil assumes responsibility for the Ministry of Modernization, he immediately begins to sell monopolies and buy influence. Furthermore, when the dust of the revolution settles and the League of Nations names Azania as a joint protectorate of France and Britain, the British diplomatic corps takes the most cynical view of "justice," determining to exile Connolly, who is the only character steadfastly loyal to Seth, but, according to the English, the "last sort of fellow one wants hanging about." Having banished Connolly to satisfy the French, the British then decide to award ownership of a disabled truck to the Azanian who has set up housekeeping in it in order to ". . . give the natives a respect for British justice."

The parallels between Waugh's experience as a reporter covering the coronation of Ras Taferi (later known as Haile Selassie) in 1930 and the events of *Black Mischief* are many. In *Remote People*, a travel book written about his experiences covering the coronation, Waugh reported the story that "the real heir to the throne was hidden in the mountains fettered with chains of solid gold." In *Black Mischief* Achon, the real heir, is indeed hidden in the mountains, although the composition of the chain escapes comment. The problems of railway travel from Djibouti to Addis Ababa reported in *Remote People*—the washing out of the lines, the tearing up of the rails for steel to make spearheads, the attacks by the natives—reappear in *Black Mischief* in the description of the trip inland on the national railway, the Grand Chemin de Fer d'Azanie.

While traveling in *Remote People*, Waugh met "two formidable ladies in knitted suits and topees; though unrelated by blood, long companionship had made them almost indistinguishable, square jawed, tight lipped, with hard, discontented eyes." The two reappear in *Black Mischief* as Dame Mildred and Miss Tin, who "were in no way related to each other but constant companionship and a similarity of interests had so characterized them that a stranger might easily have taken them to be sisters. . . each had smoked spectacles and a firm mouth."

Nowhere, however, is the parallel more distinct than in the discription of the coronation mass and ceremony itself. In *Remote People*, Waugh wrote, "The six succeeding days of celebration were to be predominantly military, but the coronation day itself was in the hands of the Church, and they were going to make the most of it." In *Black Mischief*: "The Church party were in the ascendent at the moment and were not disposed to forego a single liturgical luxury." Of the diplomats in *Remote People*, he observed that they "shifted uncomfortably in their gilt chairs," and in *Black Mischief* that "a long time passed and the diplomat shifted from buttock to buttock in his gilt chair." Achon himself is carried over from *Remote People* where "the Emperor and Empress, crowned, shuffling along under a red and gold canopy" is the orginal version of "Then a canopy of brocade supported on poles at each corner by the four premier peers of the Empire. Under it shuffled the new monarch in robes of state."

The extent to which Waugh drew on his travel books as sources of material can provide some interesting insight into the way he worked. Clearly he was able to observe the world closely and to see in all kinds of events—domestic, foreign, base, and dignified—grist for his satiric mill. One would be wrong, however, to conclude that Waugh simply drew his novels from life. In every case, the selection of incidents, their transformation, and their structuring takes the activity beyond a simple describing of incidents and characters from life. This case is fairly easily made. A far more dangerous error into which such an observation might lead the reader, however, is the assumption that when Waugh drew material from his travel books for his novels, he was then writing novels about the countries to which he had traveled. This is almost never true. Waugh is always an Englishman writing about Englishmen. In *Black Mischief*, Azania may provide the landscape, but English attitudes and English comic characters provide the humor, most of which is at their expense. A satirist does not so easily change targets.

Stylistically, Waugh made some important progress between *Vile Bodies* and *Black Mischief*. In his earlier novels, there are episodes of authorial intrusion. Unnecessarily afraid that his readers would fail to draw the conclusion he had made inescapable, Waugh would occasionally abandon his oblique narrative stance and speak directly to the reader. In *Black Mischief*, however, that sort of error seems not to occur. Rather, Waugh has learned to trust the Firbankian, farcical, fragmentary presentation he has been practicing. It is the manipulation and juxtaposition of the fragments, the disappearance of a thread of narrative and its resurfacing in later scenes, that make the action seem to move so quickly and to be so funny. If humor is partially a result of unexpected connections, Waugh's technique contributes as much to his success as his subject matter and his worldview. It is not just that he can turn a phrase; he also knows in what company it must be found to be effective.

The technique that Waugh mastered on the level of the phrase he also mastered on the level of the novel as a whole. Structurally, the novel is tidily made. In the first three chapters the three major groups of characters are introduced. In the remaining chapters, the scenes shift quickly, juxtaposing the groups to one another in all imaginable permutations, with the actions of each group casting its own particular light on the actions of the others.

3

Innocents Abroad

With the publication of *A Handful of Dust* in 1934, Waugh left behind forever the madcap, anarchical approach of his youth and began to narrow his focus. Specifically, he became increasingly concerned with tradition and with the importance of a respect for the past to the happiness of humanity. In *A Handful of Dust, Scoop,* and *Put Out More Flags,* one sees Waugh considering and rejecting a variety of secular consolations for modern man's loss of his ties to the past and the certainties it represented.

In each of these novels, there is a clear sense that something important is about to come to an end. In *A Handful of Dust* one sees most directly how the progress of the twentieth century is going to change the culture of the English country family. The code is changing, the values are changing, their lives are changing—and not for the better. In *Scoop* and *Put Out More Flags,* however, Waugh broadens his vision and sees that it is not just his world but the whole world that is changing. Furthermore, he sees that the changes are of such magnitude that it is no longer possible to dream that society can return to the golden time before the first world war. World War II made irrevocable the political and economic changes that marked the end of an epoch.

A Handful of Dust

When *A Handful of Dust* first appeared in 1934, it met with generally positive but curiously attenuated reviews. In general, the reviewers thought the book was a success, but it was so unlike the manic comedy of the three novels preceding it that the reviewers evaluated it in a tone almost of regret. In the *Times Literary Supplement*, an anonymous reviewer observed of Waugh, "Whether his study of futility is worth doing—and doing at such length—is a matter of opinion; but there can be nothing but praise for his consistency of outlook and for the grasp of purpose which rejects not only all details that might conflict with it, but any word that might be used by a shocked or sympathetic observer."[1]

Peter Quennell, writing for the *New Statesman*, noted that ". . .*A Handful of Dust*, if not the most exhilarating, is certainly the most mature and the best written novel that Mr. Waugh has yet produced."[2] This was a prescient remark, for by now many critics agree that *A Handful of Dust* is Waugh's masterpiece.

Tony Last is a young Englishman who is happily married to the lovely Lady Brenda St. Cloud with whom he has a young son and heir, John Andrew. Their home is Hetton Abbey, a large, inconvenient, and architecturally insignificant country house, which Tony loves and Brenda tolerates. For no particular reason, Brenda begins an affair with John Beaver, an unemployed advertising man who spends his days by the telephone waiting for last-minute invitations to dine out. Although friends and relatives know of Brenda's affair, Tony does not discover it until Brenda leaves him following the death of their child.

It is decided that the proper thing is to allow Brenda to divorce Tony, so he hires a woman to pose as his corespondent and goes to Brighton for the weekend with her, her eight-year-old daughter, and two employees of his lawyer to fabricate the evidence of his unfaithfulness. When Brenda attempts to renegotiate the divorce settlement upon which they had agreed and asks Tony for such a great amount of alimony that he would have to sell Hetton to provide it, she finally has gone too far, and he announces his intention to go abroad for six months, to return and divorce Brenda, and to provide no settlement for her at all.

Looking for an appropriate trip for a man waiting a decent interval for a divorce, Tony meets Dr. Messinger, an explorer who is organizing an expedition in search of a lost city in South America. Tony joins the expedition. In the South American interior they are deserted by their Indian guides, they lose their supplies, and Tony is stricken by fever. Dr. Messinger tries to go for help, but he drowns in the river, and Tony is alone in the jungle. He finds his way to the settlement of Mr. Todd, an illiterate lunatic who combines the worst features of both his European and his Indian ancestors. He cures Tony's fever but contrives to keep him, essentially a captive, making him read and reread aloud the works of Charles Dickens.

Eventually Tony is declared dead, Brenda remarries (but someone respectable, not Beaver), and Tony's impecunious cousins move into Hetton where they raise rabbits and foxes and dream of restoring the place to the splendor of cousin Tony's time.

Waugh's success with the periodical press in the years preceding *A Handful of Dust* resulted in the somewhat unusual publication history of the novel. In 1933—just back from the jungles of South America where he had gone to gather material for another travel book—Waugh published a short story, "The Man Who Liked Dickens," in *Nash's Pall Mall Magazine*. This story is essentially the penultimate chapter of *A Handful of Dust* with the exception of a few details. When *Harper's Bazaar* indicated a wish to publish the novel as a serial in the June through October issues, copyright problems associated with reprinting the story in another magazine moved Waugh to write a second ending to the novel. Thus the novel exists in two forms, one published serially and one in book form, though there is no question that the book version in which Tony remains trapped in the Brazilian jungle reading Dickens to a madman is artistically superior to the serial version.

Discussing this stage in Waugh's development is difficult because one has to acknowledge that Waugh was becoming increasingly serious in his themes without implying that he was becoming solemn. *A Handful of Dust* is not a solemn novel; rather, it is fairly consistently comical or even farcical. Even when Tony's situation is at its most moving, for example, when his son has died and he is waiting for Brenda to come home, Waugh sits him down to play a game of Animal Snap with Mrs. Rattery, and so he is found by the servants. At least he has the good sense to realize he looks ridiculous.

The differences between *A Handful of Dust* and the works preceding it, then, cannot be explained by saying they are funny and it is not. In the first three novels, however, Waugh was like a clown with an inexhaustible supply of cream pies, and he rushed around hitting every ready target he could find. Although the assumptions and institutions attacked in all three novels are related, the consistency is more a result of their all being products of the same mind rather than a result of his having a particular social or philosophical program. His general theme is simply the decline of western culture, and he gleefully points out the evidence that supports his thesis all around him.

In *A Handful of Dust*, however, the satire begins to become more focused and thus more devastating. Rather than simply pointing out all the weaknesses and inconsistencies, foolishness and petty chicanery that modern man is heir to, Waugh begins to develop some consistent themes and some positive ideas of how things ought to be different. For the first time he attempts to move beyond "English character parts" and to work out a new theme. As he explained to his friend Henry Yorke, he was now writing about "Gothic man in the hands of savages."[3]

Like all Waugh heroes, Tony Last is destined to be alone in the world, and the initial loss of his family and friends simply symbolizes the total estrangement of modern man from his society and his world. Tony is different from Paul, Adam, Seth, and Basil, however, in that he is the first of Waugh's protagonists whose character reveals any depth or complexity. He is, finally, a hero about whom the reader can care, at least a little. In creating Tony, however, Waugh took care not to make him too sympathetic. Tony, too, has his faults: naïveté, sentimentality, and a mindless acceptance of forms.

Throughout the novel, Tony is an exile in his own land because he, like Seth, is always imaginatively living in a world remote from the one inhabited by his friends and acquaintances. Their world, the world of chromium plate on walls, modern conveniences that are not convenient, and an eye to the main chance at all times, is recognizable from earlier Waugh novels. It is the world of postwar London. The world Tony loves is a little more difficult to pin down, but its clearest expression is to be found in his house, Hetton.

Waugh clearly had Hetton in mind as a symbol of what is wrong with the way Tony sees the world, for he imagined the house as an architectural monstrosity. He wrote to his friend Tom Driberg about the novel, "the frontispiece might amuse you. I instructed the architect to design the worst possible 1860 and I think he has done well."[4] In the novel, a similar aesthetic judgment is expressed by the county guidebook which describes Hetton as "entirely rebuilt in 1864 and . . . . now devoid of interest." The Gothic, or false medieval, character of Hetton Abbey and Tony's love for the interior and the exterior of this structure "devoid of interest" establishes that his place is in another, earlier world. He loves

the line of its battlements against the sky;. . . the ecclesiastical gloom of the great hall, its ceiling groined and painted in diapers of red and gold, supported on shafts of polished granite with carved capitals, half-lit by day through lancet windows of armorial stained glass, at night by a vast gasolier of brass and wrought iron, wired now and fitted with twenty electric bulbs;. . .the bedrooms with their brass bedsteads, each with a frieze of Gothic text, each named from Malory, Yseult, Elaine, Modred and Merlin, Gawaine and Bedivere, Lancelot, Perceval, Tristram, Galahad, his own dressing room, Morgan le Fay, and Brenda's Guinevere.

What is sad is that the world for which Tony longs and the one his house represents for him never really existed. Hetton is, after all, false medieval and is inextricably tied to the Arthurian legends, not to history. Furthermore, although it is called Hetton Abbey and although the great hall is characterized by "ecclesiastical gloom," the house is secularized, as the Arthurian names for the bedrooms indicate.

The aspects of Hetton Abbey that Tony loves, then, are manifestations of empty forms. Like his more modern friends and acquaintances, Tony values surfaces and appearances; the main difference between him and Mrs. Beaver is that he loves old surfaces and she loves new ones. Hetton Abbey is both old and old-fashioned compared to the designs of chromium and glass favored by Mrs. Beaver, but it is no less devoid of values. As Tony misvalues Hetton simply because it is old, Waugh suggests that when he looks to the past for moral guidance he will misvalue what he sees there as well.

Because Tony is closely identified with his house, the emptiness of the forms connected with the house suggest that other parts of Tony's life may be empty as well, and indeed they are. Take his Sunday morning activity, for example: he always attends church, planning to hear a sermon he knows will be irrelevant to himself and his neighbors; during the service, which is intended to make one think spiritual thoughts, he thinks about remodeling his house; after the service he drinks a glass of sherry "rather solemnly" in the library. In all, he appears to enjoy the routine for itself rather than for the values symbolized by the earlier days he thinks he copies. As the narrator observes, Tony's activities are a "simple, mildly ceremonious order of his Sunday morning, which had evolved, more or less spontaneously, from the more severe practices of his parents." Thus Waugh sets the stage to reveal just how empty forms can be when Tony says of his son's death, "After all the last thing one wants to talk about at a time like this is religion."

Throughout the novel Tony attempts to observe the forms, to do things as they are supposed to be done, in an attempt to maintain some order in his world. He agrees to let Brenda divorce him even though she is the one who has been unfaithful with the result that he very nearly loses his estate and can save it only by giving up the idea of "doing the right thing" about the divorce. He decides to go abroad to recover because that seems like the proper thing to do. On the voyage he becomes romantically involved with a young Catholic woman, which is not the proper thing to do, and, of course, he ultimately finds himself in the hands of Mr. Todd. Because the forms are empty and essentially meaningless, they are no more effective in providing a moral center than the more obviously flawed forms observed by Mrs. Beaver and Polly Cockpurse.

Again and again, it appears that the characters will do the right thing, the action will be resolved, and order will be reasserted. Every time, however, the attempt to restore order falters and chaos reigns. Mrs. Rattery, Jock's Shameless Blonde, and her perpetual game of four-deck patience provide a good central symbol of the tension between order and chaos. She spends inordinate amounts of time "moving little groups of cards adroitly backward and forwards about the table like shuttles across a loom; under her fingers order grew out of chaos; she established sequence and precedence; the symbols before her became coherent, interrelated." Even the competent Mrs. Rattery, however, cannot establish order in a world governed by chance, and when all the pieces will not fit, chaos triumphs: "Mrs. Rattery brooded over her chequer of cards and then drew them toward her into a heap, haphazard once more and without meaning; it had nearly come to a solution that time, but for a six of diamonds out of place, and a stubbornly congested patch at one corner, where nothing could be made to move. 'It's a heartbreaking game,' she said." Like Mrs. Rattery's cards, a decent man's life often seems almost to work out, and then collapses. Life, the novel says, like Mrs. Rattery's game of patience, is heartbreaking.

Although Tony's values can make no more sense of the world than the values of his London friends, it is clear that he is the moral center of the novel and that we are to be more concerned with Tony's well-being than with the others. His moral code may not be sufficient to save him, but he is plainly a far more decent person than anyone else in the novel. He has a code and, like Paul Pennyfeather, he is proud of it. But the novel illustrates again and again the ineffectiveness of the old code, romantic and chivalric as it is, in the modern world. The reference to the Arthurian legends reminds one that the old code was not all that successful in the world Tony longs for, either. Like Tony, King Arthur was betrayed by both his wife and his best friend. Tony's trusting his wife does not keep her faithful; his acceptance of her word as bond in the settlement agreement does not keep her from reneging; and his conviction that Mr. Todd can be talked to as a man of reason and honor probably accounts for Mr. Todd's drugging him when rescuers approach. In short, it is Tony's romanticism, his tendency to idealize, that makes him more admirable than the others even as it leads to his downfall.

Like all of his predecessors except Basil Seal, Tony is an example of modern man excluded from his world. Thus he shares with earlier heroes the status of victim. In Tony Last, however, Waugh has introduced a new kind of protagonist. For the first time, he presents an innocent who initiates a strategy of withdrawal. Also for the first time, withdrawal does not provide the hero with the protection he seeks. Tony's strategy of sequestering himself in his country home with his family fails to protect him from involvement with the "savages" to which the modern world calls him.

The flaw in Tony's scheme is the lack of a positive faith on which he can base his withdrawal. He withdraws on the basis of empty forms rather than positive commitment. For example, he is committed to the form of attending church on Sunday, but not to the religious ideas that, at least in theory, underlie church activities. Thus, when his son is killed, he can say, "Religion is the last thing one wants to think of in a time like this."

In the tragic quality of Tony's existence, mixed as it is with the comic shenanigans of Brenda's London friends, the reader perceives Waugh's understanding of the senselessness of attempts to provide secular answers to important problems. Tony's end—exile in the hands of a lunatic in the jungle—is even more horrible than Seth's murder by his erstwhile subjects. But Tony has tried as hard as Paul Pennyfeather to live by his code. The problem is that Tony's code, the code of the nineteenth-century gentleman, is not only anachronistic but destructive. In Waugh's vision, the code has moved from being irrelevant to being dangerous. Secular humanism, the attitude that leads Tony to value his house, his traditions, and his family above all else, cannot provide a context within which even a decent man can find a livable life. He can withdraw behind such bulwarks, but they will not protect him from the savages.

If Tony is Gothic man, an 1860 revival of a twelfth century construct, who are the savages? Most obviously, the savages are the inhabitants of the South American jungle who desert the expedition and the ghoulish Mr. Todd who holds Tony captive. Waugh builds carefully to his climax, however, by introducing several other groups of savages along the way.

The first group of savages are the members of London society with whom Brenda falls in and to whom she introduces Mr. Beaver. Interested only in what is new, and lacking any other touchstone, the London tribe accepts and encourages childish and self-centered behavior within the group. It accepts and, indeed, encourages marital infidelity; for example, when Brenda takes up with John Beaver, she and her friends send Jenny Akbar, one of their circle, to Hetton Abbey in hopes that Tony will have an affair with her.

The second group of savages are the people with whom Tony is driven to associate in order to organize the evidence for his divorce. His corespondent, her daughter, the professional witnesses, the other residents of the tawdry seaside hotel are all something less than civilized and something more than threatening to the moral order of a society. Brenda's brother Reggie must also be included in this group that might be called the divorce tribe, for it is he who articulates what the others only enact—the principle that modern man can no longer "afford" traditional values.

Beside the depredations of these two groups, the activities of the actual South American Indians seem very nearly benign. They are childlike and credulous, but their abandonment of Tony and their refusal to help him in the search for his idealized city is no different from the betrayals of his English friends. When he comes to the home of Mr. Todd, to the truly horrifying death-in-life of his jungle existence, Waugh has found a perfect correlative for the spiritual death-in-life that is the fate of modern man. As was true of Azania in *Black Mischief*, Brazil is important in *A Handful of Dust* less for what it tells the reader about conditions in South America than for what it tells the reader of conditions in England.

Tony's decision to leave England and to travel with Dr. Messinger in search of a lost city is, for Tony, a way to try to find a part of the modern world in which ancient values live. For Waugh, it is an opportunity to recapitulate in different terms the same theme he has sounded in the London and Brighton scenes of the novel. The lost city, called by the Indians "the Shining, the Many Watered, the Bright Feathered" comes to replace Hetton Abbey as the symbol of Tony's idealization of the past. Its Indian names suggest fertility and growth and make the city seem to be the fount of life. Tony's decision to search for the city, then, becomes a symbolic decision to search for life in the face of the spiritual death civilization has brought to him. When he pictures the city in his mind, he sees

vanes and pinnacles, gargoyles, battlements, groining and tracery, pavilions and terraces, a transfigured Hetton, pennons and banners floating on the sweet breeze, everything luminous and translucent; a coral citadel crowning a green hill top sewn with daisies, among groves and streams; a tapestry landscape filled with heraldic and fabulous animals and symmetrical, disproportionate blossom.

It is a landscape, one might say, absolutely Arthurian and with far more relation to the mythic history of Britain than to the ancient civilizations of Brazil. For Tony, however, the city is a sanctuary, a place where he will find comfort and protection from his enemies.

Tony has no greater success in finding what he is searching for in Brazil than he has had in England, however, and instead of the city he finds the squalid, ant-ridden homestead of Mr. Todd, who, in a way like Tony, is determined to resist the future. In him one sees how destructive to oneself and to others such a determination can be. Instead of an Arthurian hero who dispenses justice and rewards virtue, Tony finds a madman who twists every good thing—the cross, healing, literature—to a bad end.

Scoop

Like the novels preceding *A Handful of Dust, Scoop* is pure comedy. Reviewers from the *Tablet* to the *Times Literary Supplement* to the *Daily Telegraph* had little but praise for Waugh's "ribald wit,"[5] his "inventive talent, his intelligence, [and] the flexibility of his prose."[6] More than once reviewers remarked with admiration on Waugh's ability to satirize without resorting to invective or displaying bad temper.[7]

In *Scoop*, Waugh again draws upon his experiences in Ethiopia, formerly Abyssinia, this time placing his novel in Ishmaelia, a small country on the coast of northeast Africa. The novel opens, however, in London where John Boot, a successful young novelist, is asking his lovely and influential friend Mrs. Stitch to help him find a job that will take him out of the country. When Mrs. Stitch convinces Lord Copper, publisher of the daily newspaper the *Beast* that "Boot is your man" to cover the seemingly inevitable civil war in Ishmaelia, Lord Copper takes her advice. However, his confused foreign editor hires William Boot, a young country gentleman who writes a weekly nature column for *The Beast* called "Lush Places."

Despite his reluctance to leave his home, William is persuaded by the foreign editor to go to Ishmaelia as a war correspondent. Outfitted with every piece of equipment that the most creative supplier could imagine, including a dozen cleft sticks for sending in news dispatches, William embarks for Ishmaelia. En route he meets a mysterious Englishman who is distinguished by his hair color: "a strong purplish shade of auburn."

The Republic of Ishmaelia has been ruled for the forty years of its existence by the Jackson family; however, when William arrives, a challenge to the Jackson family has arisen. Like Lord Copper, other publishers throughout the world have sent reporters to cover this challenge to authority.

In Jacksonburg, the capital city, William meets and falls in love with Katchen, a young Russian/German/Pole whose husband has left her stranded with no money and a satchel full of rocks. She sells the rocks to William who discovers that they contain gold. Ishmaelia is rich in mineral wealth and the "civil war" is in fact a contest between the Germans and the Russians for control of this resource.

The mysterious auburn-haired Englishman reappears to "protect vital British interests" in the country. Covering this story while all the other journalists are out of town on a government-organized wild goose chase, William scores a worldwide scoop. He returns to London lionized and is offered a knighthood. All he wants, however, is to go home and to have his old column, "Lush Places," back. So the knighthood is given to John Boot, who regards it as ample compensation for Mrs. Stitch's earlier failure to act on his behalf.

As is always the case with Waugh, a sketch such as this suggests nothing of the charm of the novel, for the charm is not in the story to be told, but in the telling. It is Waugh's eye for details and incidents that can be exaggerated into absurdity and his ability to do the exaggerating with a perfectly straight face that make *Scoop* so much fun.

William, like his predecessors, is in exile; but William's exile is self-imposed. He deliberately withdraws from the world, dislikes being forced into it, and retreats when he gets the chance. Like Tony Last, he wants to remain at home in the midst of a small circle of family and other members of the household. For reasons not structurally clear but probably having to do with his own personal happiness (he married Laura Herbert in 1937), Waugh was able to manage in *Scoop* a vision of a world in which an innocent could hold his own when he was forced into public and yet could retire at will. Still, in the final image of owls hunting maternal rodents and their furry brood, he acknowledges that William's victory is not necessarily permanent and that even those who attempt to stay out of the line of fire may be in some danger. *Scoop*, then, is a comic vision of the world of Tony Last. Tony and William have much in common, but in one important fact they differ: William inhabits a congenial universe.

The title *Scoop* suggests that the focus of the novel is on journalism, and the suggestion is accurate. Having used his experiences as a schoolboy, a university student, and a schoolmaster to focus *Decline and Fall* on educational institutions; his experience as a young novelist about town to focus on the bright young things of *Vile Bodies*; his sad experiences as a betrayed husband to focus on the despair of Tony Last; and his experience as a travel writer to look at Azania in *Black Mischief*; Waugh turned to his brief career as a journalist to provide a focus for the fun in *Scoop*. His career, it should be said, was not at all like William's; it was really rather more like that of the boy Bateson who was hired "on space" as a favor to a correspondence school that advertised in the *Beast*.

One of the reasons critics are often reluctant to describe Waugh's work as satire is that it very often seems not to be interested in setting things right. *Scoop* is a case in point. One cannot say that Waugh has a vision of how journalism ought to be practiced that he intends to promote by pointing out how badly it *is* practiced. Instead he seems content simply to collect examples of the foibles of journalists and to embellish them until they appear to be examples of pure madness.

For example, Lord Copper, publisher of the *Beast*, is a parody of the successful businessman who behaves as if success has ensured his infallibility when instead it has simply broadened his opportunities to make a fool of himself. Like his banquets, Lord Copper is "a little over life-size, unduly large." His success gives him leave to pontificate in public when he chooses; at Margot Metroland's party, Lord Copper seizes the opportunity:

"The workings of a great newspaper," said Lord Copper, feeling at last thoroughly Rotarian, "are of a complexity which the public seldom appreciates. The citizen little realizes the vast machinery put into motion in exchange for his morning penny." ("Oh God," said Lady Metroland, faintly but audibly.)

The pure pleasure that Lord Copper takes in his cliche-ridden, bombastic speech is the source of much of the humor in his character.

In addition to being pompous, Lord Copper is wonderfully, amazingly impetuous and liable to demonstrate real lack of judgment. Mrs. Stitch says "hire Boot." Lord Copper says "hire Boot [of whom he has never heard] at any price." This characteristic provides opportunities for one of Waugh's favorite humorous methods—he lets his character make a statement in a way that shows he has hit a sore spot, then he lets the narrator explain why the spot is sore. Lord Copper exhorts his editor to hire Boot "at any price":

"Well, at any reasonable price," he added, for there had lately been a painful occurrence when instructions of this kind, given in an expan-

sive mood, had been too literally observed and a trick cyclist, who
had momentarily attracted Lord Copper's attention, had been engaged
to edit the Sports Page on a five years' contract at five thousand a
year.

Like Lord Copper, the editors of the *Beast* come in for rid-
icule. Where Lord Copper's humor is his overconfidence, theirs
is their overcautiousness, born of fear and trembling. They are
agreeable to the point of being willing to re-create reality in
order to avoid angering Lord Copper. For example, Mr. Salter's
obsequiousness is illustrated in his inability to disagree with his
employer even about simple matters of fact:

> "Let me see, what's the name of the place I mean? Capital of
> Japan? Yokohama, isn't it?"
> "Up to a point, Lord Copper."
> "And Hong Kong belongs to us, doesn't it?"
> "Definitely, Lord Copper."

In addition to being yes men, the editors are profoundly
ignorant of almost everything, and *Scoop* suggests that the
profession is structured to make sure they stay that way. Mr.
Salter, the foreign editor of the *Beast*, began his career selecting
jokes for a publication called *Clean Fun*; from there he moved to
"the ruthless, cut-throat, rough-and-tumble of the *Beast* Woman's
Page. From there, crushed and bedraggled, he had been tossed
into the editorial chair of the Imperial and Foreign News." Thus
it is that when William meets him, Mr. Salter is looking at an
atlas in which he "had been vainly trying to find Reykjavík."

As publishers are pompous and editors are ignorant, reporters in *Scoop* are impostors. They cheat on their expense accounts; they resort to petty chicanery to scoop one another;
and they make up news when they can't find anything real to
report. In short, they will do anything for a scoop, even if the
news they report is imaginary.

One of the superb turns Waugh does on the irresponsibility of the press is Corker's story of the famous Wenlock Jakes. Jakes was on his way to cover a revolution when he fell asleep in the train and missed his stop. Awakening later, he left the train, not realizing that he was in the wrong country. He went directly to his hotel and, although the country in which he had disembarked was at peace, he began to file story after story about the devastation resulting from the revolution: "Government stocks dropped, financial panic, state of emergency declared, army mobilized, famine, mutiny—and in less than a week there was an honest to God revolution under way."

Jakes's rival among the crew sent to Ishmaelia is Sir Jocelyn Hitchcock, who is too busy writing a book of memoirs to be called *Under the Ermine* actually to cover any of the events at hand. His introduction is a model of the chatty, gossipy, awestruck style of the American who worships the aristocracy:

> I shall never forget the evening of King Edward's abdication. I was dining at the Savoy Grill as the guest of Silas Shock of the *New York Guardian*. His guests were well chosen; six of the most influential men and women in England, who are seldom in the news but who control the strings of the national pulse. . . . I at once raised the question of the hour. Not one of that brilliant company expressed any opinion. There in a nutshell, you have *England*, her greatness—and her littleness.

In addition to the emptiness of the rhetoric (there is absolutely no information in the entire paragraph), Hitchcock's writing is characterized by a complete lack of logic. What, one may ask, are "the strings of the national pulse"?

Sir Jocelyn is also famous for his firsthand account of an earthquake in Messina that he covered without ever leaving London. Shumble, a British newsman, creates a Soviet agent out of the advance man for William's auburn-haired Englishman and is credited with a world scoop. Olafsen, the Swedish correspondent, liberates the imprisoned President Jackson by getting blind drunk on absinthe and driving the leader of the Young Ishmaelites off the balcony in the middle of his announcement of a successful coup. In all, the reporters are presented as impostors and clowns.

Reporters are also fiercely competitive, mouthing solidarity and cooperation, and cutting one another's throats at every opportunity. For example, when William receives his first telegram, he is confused by the language: OPPOSITION SPLASHING FRONTWARD SPEEDILIEST STOP ADEN REPORTED WARWISE FLASH FACTS BEAST. It appears to William that the only sensible part of the message is "STOP ADEN," which he takes to mean that he should remain in Aden, and Corker allows him to believe that is correct. It is not until Corker receives a message that he and William are on the same team that he translates the message for the novice and reveals that waiting in Aden would be exactly the wrong thing to do.

The same willingness to betray one another in the name of fair and free competition is manifest in the press corps' preparation to visit the interior of Ishmaelia and the nonexistent city of Laku. Everyone talks of "making a move at tennish," but nearly the entire corps is up and on the move at dawn, trying to secure the advantage of a few hours start. Unfortunately for the corps, there are more impenetrable obstacles to "fair and free competition" than cheating one's friends, and one of them is the Ishmaelian night guard who arrests the whole group, delaying their departure until after the ten o'clock opening of the press bureau. For Waugh then the entire journalistic establishment is subject to posturing, pretension, and pure dishonesty.

Like most of Waugh's novels, *Scoop* is circular in structure; it begins with William at Boot Magna, sends him out into the world, and brings him back home. However, it is not the case that Boot Magna represents a haven from the madness of Lon don and Ishmaelia. The world of Boot Magna is as potty as one can imagine: The house and grounds are in a state of advanced disrepair—some simply from the passage of time and some representing a decline in the ability to keep the world orderly. Waugh makes the physical world of Boot Magna parallel the decline of humanity. Notice how the trees become human in his description:

The immense trees which encircled Boot Magna Hall, shaded its drives and rides, and stood (tastefully disposed at the whim of some forgotten, provincial predecessor of Repton) singly and in groups about the park, had suffered, some from ivy, some from lightening, some from the various malignant disorders that vegetation is heir to, but all, principally, from old age. Some were supported with trusses and crutches of iron.

Not only has the physical world become decrepit, it has become chaotic. The lake is sometimes an "opaque pool in a wilderness of mud and rushes," and sometimes an expanse of open water covering five acres of pastureland. Although William loves it, even nature is not to be trusted.

Inside Boot Magna Hall, the inhabitants are as ancient and unpredictable as the water system and the trees. The household comprises eight Boots, eight old family retainers (most of whom are confined to bed and require a great deal of attention from the family), and ten servants who spend most of their waking hours eating "the five meat meals which tradition daily allowed them."

The Boots of Boot Magna Hall are best described as "decayed gentlefolk." They are eccentric, oblivious to the world around them, and monomaniacal. As Mr. Salter learns at dinner, each of the Boots functions independently, even at table:

before each plate was ranged a little store of seasonings and delicacies, all marked with their owner's initials—onion salt, Bombay duck, gherkins, garlic vinegar, Dijon mustard, peanut butter, icing sugar, varieties of biscuit from Bath and Tunbridge Wells, Parmesan cheese, and a dozen other jars and bottles and tins.

The monomaniacal quality of the Boots household is part of the comic atmosphere of the novel. Priscilla cares only for horses, Uncle Theodore for telling smutty stories, and Nanny Bloggs for making a shilling or two by gambling, whether at dominoes, at bridge, or at playing the ponies. In fact, one of the qualities that quite sets William apart in the novel is that when he is removed from Boot Magna Hall, he loses his monomaniacal quality and does not regain it until he returns home.

At Boot Magna Hall, William is completely at rest and completely willing to remain so. He longs for little except to remain in the "Lush Places" and to avoid any embarrassment in the eyes of his friends and acquaintances. Although the reader has the narrator's word that William has always longed to fly (that is, that the urge to transcend the ordinary arises in him), what one really sees is his desire to remain at rest. His being summoned to London is traumatic for him, as is his being assigned to Ishmaelia. His love for Katchen is obviously incompatible with the life he has chosen at Boot Magna, for she has no roots while William has more than he can really transcend.

Where Katchen has no clearly defined national origin (her husband is German, her father is Russian, her mother is Polish), William's family have lived in the same house on the same grounds since the eighteenth century (when some "provincial predecessor of Repton" designed the park). In fact, William's Uncle Bernard has traced the line all the way back to Aethelred the Unready. Like his ancestor, William is remarkably unready for the cycle of events in which he finds himself involved. Of course, anyone would be; for a world in which William can be summoned to London and then sent to Ishmaelia is too unpredictable to allow us to hold anyone really responsible for his actions.

This is the wonderful irony of Waugh's method of composition. His sense of structure is so highly developed that incidents that seem to be totally unrealistic—i.e., fanciful or farcical in terms of the probability of their happening in a rational world—are inevitable in terms of the structure. He makes the unforeseeable seem to be preordained.

While William is in the world, however, he loses his static quality and takes action in the world as the hero of a romantic novel or an adventure story might be expected to do. For instance, throughout the novel, people keep trying to make William move. First Salter bullies him by saying that if William doesn't agree to go to Ishmaelia, he will be fired. Then Mr. Benito tries to send him into the interior. In Ishmaelia, however, William is capable of asserting himself and making others capitulate. Mr. Benito cannot make him go to Laku: " 'Oh, rot,' said William. 'For one thing there is no such place as Laku.' " Even the welterweight champion of the Adventist University of Alabama, who comes to pressure William to sell Katchen's gold-bearing mineral samples cannot make him move.

Although he can refuse to move in Ishmaelia, William is not static there. On the contrary, he is able to make the decisions and take the actions that make him a romance hero (though of a very ironic kind) while he is away from home. Like a fairy tale hero, William is nothing without his friends—his first big story is based on the gossip Katchen hears from the president's governess. His second big story is written in the heroic mode—Waugh describes William as if he were a real hero fighting a real battle: "He foresaw a spectacular, cinematographic consummation, when his country should rise chivalrously to arms: Bengal Lancers and kilted Highlanders invested the heights of Jacksonburg; he at their head burst open the prison doors." More important, however, the information upon which this heroic tale is based comes from his friend Bannister.

The third story, garnered from the experiences of Katchen's

"husband," is written by William but transmitted only by the intervention of the "god from the machine," Mr. Baldwin. And the final story in which all the pieces are pulled together with an undeniably romantic cast given to them is not only based on Mr. Baldwin's information but is actually composed by him: "Mr. Baldwin sat at William's table and drew the typewriter towards himself. He inserted a new sheet of paper, tucked up his cuffs and began to write with immense speed."

William, like Tony Last, is an essentially decent, well-educated, sensitive English gentleman. He is not lucky in love (nor is Tony), but then neither is any other Waugh hero. He is, however, surely better than most people in the novel—more sensitive, kinder, more honest, and more innocent. To be out of the world is not a bad thing for him, for he is almost too innocent to live in it. However, his innocence, his naïveté, and his innate decency combine to make him more successful in the world than most of the characters around him. In a very pragmatic sense, he is the most successful of the journalists in Ishmaelia, and in the wider view of the novel he is undoubtedly successful, for he manages to retain the right to do what he wants to do. He goes home; he continues to write his column; and he doesn't embarrass himself before Nanny Bloggs. One could say that like Paul Pennyfeather, he learns not to participate in life. On the other hand, one could conclude that the novel counsels as follows: The world is a dangerous place ("Outside the owls hunted maternal rodents and their furry broods"), but even so it is not utterly untenable. There is a future, and one that may be anticipated with pleasure.

Thus *Scoop* is among the most positive of Waugh's novels. Even more than *Decline and Fall*, *Scoop* presents a world that is mad without being malevolent, chaotic without being meaningless. It is, in fact, a richly comic world in which characters are rewarded in accordance with what they want rather than what they deserve—even if what they want is a little mad itself. In this generous spirit Waugh forsees "a future for Lord Copper that was full to surfeit of things which no sane man seriously coveted."

Put Out More Flags

In *Put Out More Flags*, the bright young people of Waugh's earlier novels, now approaching middle age, finally embark upon the war that has been threatening since *Vile Bodies*. Like real people, Waugh's characters respond to the national tragedy with a sentimentalism that seems unrealistic. Alastair Digby-Vaine-Trumpington enters the armed forces as an enlisted man, as, his wife explains, "a kind of penance" for all the fun he has had. Peter Pastmaster is overcome by "pangs of dynastic conscience" and decides he should marry and have a son. The lovely Angela Lyne closes up her rooms and takes to excessive and solitary drink. No one, however, changes as dramatically as Basil Seal, who for the first time recognizes that he has overstepped the bounds of decency and who, also for the first time, seems to try to take action in the world for the benefit of someone else when he rescues Angela from her depression.

Put Out More Flags was a critical success, although some critics began to worry that, like Basil Seal, Waugh might be turning serious on them. Alan Pryce-Jones was completely positive in the *New Statesman*, saying that "*Put Out More Flags* is to be praised without any reserve so long as the author is at the attack, direct or implicit. The best of the book shows that his commando has little to teach him in the technique of the sharp destructive raid."[8] The *Saturday Review* was also full of praise, finding Waugh to be "eminently a mature artist" and asserting that "in all his novels— and I think that they are among the most original novels of our time—he has always sought to discover the *lacrimae rerum*, and we should not take him any the less seriously because he makes his discovery with a fleer."[9]

The novel has a four-part structure; the sections are entitled "Autumn," "Winter," "Spring," and "Summer," indicating another of the circular structures typical of Waugh's work. The novel is dedicated to Randolph Churchill, son of the prime minister, with an evocation of "that odd, dead period before the Churchillian renaissance" and "a race of ghosts, survivors of the world we both knew ten years ago," for by 1942, England had been at war for three years and Waugh had joined the Royal Marines. *Put Out More Flags*, Waugh said, was ". . . a minor work, dashed off in the voyage, but it has some good bits."[10]

The novel opens with the country preparing for war. Basil Seal's sister, Barbara, is at home at her country estate, Malfrey, helping her husband prepare to be mobilized with the yeomanry, trying to keep her servants from quitting because of the disruption caused by the women and children who have been evacuated to the country from Birmingham, and thinking about Basil.

Basil's mother, Lady Seal, is at home in London, remembering her dead husband and the last war, lunching with Sir Joseph Mainwaring, and thinking about Basil.

Basil's lover, Angela Lyne, is in France on a train bound for England, looking controlled and self-sufficient, contemplating death, and thinking about Basil.

In addition to the three women in Basil's life, the first section of the novel introduces a group of aesthetes, some less bogus than others. Poppet Green is a second-rate and derivative artist whose work is based on surreal images "conventionally arranged in the manner of Dali." Ambrose Silk, a contemporary of Basil and a self styled "Jewish pansy," is a writer who self-consciously belongs "to the age of the ivory tower." Poppet's friends are characterized by their long discussions of the work of Parsnip and Pimpernell, two English poets who have gone to America, and their equally long discussions of the People's Cause.

Alastair and Sonia Trumpington and Peter Pastmaster are also contemporaries of Basil. Peter, having once been in the cavalry, has a commission and is in uniform; Alastair wants a commission but is too old, so he enlists and is shipped to a training camp where Sonia later joins him.

The other major character introduced in "Autumn" is the Ministry of Information. Housed in "the vast bulk of London University," the Ministry of Information is staffed by a group of eccentrics who spend their time referring other eccentrics to each other. Ambrose Silk's publisher works there.

The "Winter" section begins when, despite Sir Joseph Mainwaring's efforts, Basil fails to secure a place in the elite Brigade of Guards and retreats to Malfrey where he discovers that Barbara is the billeting officer for the district (that is, she finds places for the appalling Birmingham evacuees to stay). In the persons of the Connollies, three extremely disagreeable and destructive children, Basil finds his ticket to becoming "one of the hard-faced men who made money out of the war." His plan is elegant in its simplicity—he simply assigns the barbarians to impossible situations and then allows the hosts to buy their ways out.

While Basil amuses himself by terrorizing Barbara's neighbors with the Connollies, the rest of the bright young people turn serious. Alastair Trumpington turns down a chance to go to an officer-training unit, glories in discovering how to shirk physical training, and learns to operate a mortar. Ambrose Silk becomes the resident atheist at the religious department of the Ministry of Information where he conceives of a new literary review, to be called the *Ivory Tower*. Angela Lyne, who regards cocktails as familiar and thus never drinks in public, begins to drink far too much in private. And Peter Pastmaster decides to marry.

In "Spring," Basil's brother-in-law Freddy is about to return to Malfrey from his training with the yeomanry. Basil, always alert, "sells" the Connollies to the billeting officer from the neighboring district and returns to London. Pressed by his mother to do *something*, he goes to the War Office to offer his services.

Choosing an office because of a pretty girl, Basil presents himself to the Assistant Deputy Director of Internal Security. He gains instant credibility by reporting the presence in the building of a mad bomber (whose entrance into the building Basil himself arranged). When the bomb goes off in the middle of his interview, he's hired.

When Angela's drinking and depression become known to Basil, he begins to spend more time with her and less time at the office. Pressed by ADDIS to justify his existence, he denounces Ambrose and his *Ivory Tower* as fascist. However, when he learns that Ambrose may really be arrested on this charge, Basil realizes that this time the game could have serious consequences, so he warns Ambrose and encourages him to assume the disguise of a priest and escape to Ireland. Basil, in his absence, takes over Ambrose's London apartment and his crepe de chine underwear.

Angela's husband, Cedric, returns to London to say goodbye, and is killed in action on his first day in battle.

Chapter 4, "Summer," is very short. In a few pages Waugh ties up all the strings. Sir Joseph Mainwaring goes right on misinterpreting everything he sees. Alastair is recruited by Peter Pastmaster to join a commando group. Angela and Basil marry, and Basil joins the commandos, too. Ambrose Silk is exiled on the west coast of Ireland, where his attempts to be creative are thwarted by the atmosphere of Ireland and of the times.

For the first time, it appears that being an exile is not a bad fate. So much is to be shunned, so little to be admired in the world of ministries of this and that, proletarian art and politics, and impending political disaster that to be out of it seems better than to be in. For Basil and his friends, all roads lead out of Eden. Angela Lyne phrases it best: "In the old days," she explains to Basil, "if there was one thing wrong it spoiled everything; from now on for all our lives, if there's one thing right the day is made."

Even his sister sees Basil as a soldier *manqué*, and thus someone outside his proper realm. We are led to believe that Barbara would be like Basil, a wild little animal and an outsider, if "maternity and Malfrey" had not domesticated her. Thus love and good classical architecture are credited with bringing Barbara into the fold. Presumably, Angela Lyne and the lovely old house called Cedric's Folly could eventually work some of the same magic on Basil, although the closing pages of the novel do not seem all that hopeful. Basil will be a terrible husband (still outside the orderly family structure), Ambrose is in Ireland, Rampole is in jail, and Sir Joseph still fails to understand what is happening in the world. Love and family may be enough to keep one going one step at a time during a blackout, but it does not seem to be enough to make the world meaningful or to allow one to be content. Throughout history people have tried to achieve a sense of oneness by submersing themselves in greater causes: war, art, literature, manifest destiny. But *Put Out More Flags* does not suggest that such secular strategies can hope to satisfy.

For Waugh, society seems to have disintegrated completely. His biographers say that by 1942 he was hopelessly disenchanted with the army and with the possibility of being a man of action. He had already questioned the possibility of being a man of letters, a married man, a modern man. In *Put Out More Flags* he suggests for the first time that the world is not only absurd for the ordinary folk but is also uncongenial to the family of jokers who found it possible to roll with the punches in the earlier novels. Waugh was accustomed to presenting an antic world in which one or two people for whom the reader cared were discomfited; in *Put Out More Flags*, however, the whole family of outsiders, who had been providing an alternating surface off which the main characters could ricochet, suddenly find themselves ill at ease. Whether they know it or not, almost all the characters are lamentably out of place now that the world has changed. Now, they are all exiles in the modern world.

Basil, for example, has become a professional enfant terrible. At the age of thirty-six, however, that is a difficult role to sustain. His friends among the younger generation call him "an old adventurer," and even his mother puts the pressure on her younger son to start a career. The ultimate repudiation of Basil's earlier life, however, is his marriage to Angela Lyne, with its suggestion of prosperity, family, settling down, and responsibility. Thus at the end of the novel, Waugh lets Basil decide to share his exile. There is, however, no suggestion that it is possible to end it.

Alastair and Sonia Trumpington, too, are exiles. Although they "always have fun," as Sonia observes, even they notice that the world has moved on without them: "Sonia would sometimes remark how odd it was that the papers nowadays never seemed to mention anyone one had ever heard of; they had been such a bore once, never leaving one alone."

Waugh is careful to point out that, at least in the eyes of his heroes and heroines, it is not they but the world that has changed. Of Sonia, he says, "Basil saw little change in her beauty now and none in the rich confusion of letters, newspapers, half-opened parcels and half-empty bottles, puppies, flowers and fruit which surrounded the bed." Peter Pastmaster assumes the role of an old dog but is only really attractive when something of the "fascinating little boy" he once was surfaces.

The best example of the exile in *Put Out More Flags*, however, is Ambrose Silk, the artist, who becomes Basil's double here just as Seth did in *Black Mischief*. From the beginning of the novel, Ambrose perceives himself as an outcast. He knows that his effeminate gestures, his giggles, and his clothes all mark him as an outsider. He is a Jew, an aesthete, a homosexual, and an atheist—that is, he manages to define himself as being outside every traditional social structure in the Western world. By the end of the novel, Ambrose is bearing almost the entire weight of Waugh's nostalgia for the prewar world. When Basil succeeds in disguising him and sending him to the west coast of Ireland to await the end of the war, he sends away what the change of times has exiled. Ambrose takes away the qualities the other characters once shared with him. In doing so, he functions as a double for the Young Turks who remain. Instead of Ambrose's finely honed epithets, modern humanity must learn to live with the monotonous obscenities of the troops and the prosaic piety of the civil servants.

What actually seems to happen throughout the novel is that each of the exiles is given an opportunity (or, perhaps, more than one) to repudiate his or her sense of separation from the "herd" and to make common cause with society. Some seize the opportunity (for longer or shorter periods of time), while others reject it completely. Ambrose, for example, feels his exile sharply but cannot bear to give it up. Atheist, homosexual, and an aesthete, he revels in his separation from all others, including other intellectuals. Thus it is particularly ironic that when Ambrose flees to Ireland, achieving the isolation he argues is appropriate to an artist, he stops producing: "The days passed and he did absolutely nothing."

For the rest of Basil's set, there is a uniform desire to return to a kind of schoolboy acceptance of association. Peter Pastmaster sets the tone most clearly: "Most of war seems to consist of hanging about," he said. "Let's at least hang about with our own friends." Alastair and Basil seem to share Peter's attitude, the boyishness of which is underlined by Alastair's continuing infatuation with weapons—he cannot bear it if Peter has a sword and he has none; he delightedly takes up the mortar because it is "one of the key points of the defense"; and he is wooed away from the mortar by the even more romantic rope ladders and knuckledusters promised him by the special service units, the commandos.

If all the erstwhile bright young people are exiles, who represents the establishment? Sir Joseph Mainwaring is surely the voice of the establishment, and he gets everything exactly wrong. More precisely, he gets it wrong in ways he could never imagine. The Ministry of Information and the War Office, not to mention the officers, who make an orderly embarkation impossible and then find that Cedric Lyne has made "a nonsense" of the exercise, represent the establishment.

What is interesting about this novel is that the roles have shifted. Although Basil is accustomed to sowing disorder wherever he goes, in *Put Out More Flags* he finds himself stunned by the disorder of the world around him—"It was like being in Latin America at a time of upheaval and, instead of being an Englishman, being oneself a Latin-American." And indeed, Basil's crowd have likewise become the conservatives. Alastair, who was long ago Margot Metroland's lover, now observes "certain immature taboos of dress, such as wearing a bowler hat in London until after Goodwood Week." Furthermore, Alastair enlists out of a simple patriotic commitment that even Waugh knows is going to sound ridiculous if he puts it into words. So he does not, and attributes his diffidence to fear of Basil.

Put Out More Flags probably seems more sensible and coherent than the novels preceding it because war is such a useful metaphor for a society that has ceased to make sense. In the early novels Waugh already thought the world was mad, but he had not at hand so strong a unifying metaphor with which to convey the idea. Here for the first time, he has a peg on which to hang the variety of indictments he has to bring against the modern world. Once having found this metaphor, he went right on using it for the rest of his life.

As *Scoop* was clearly a satire of the journalist's trade, *Put Out More Flags* is directed at the military man. By 1942 when the novel was written, Waugh, who was on his way home from the Middle East on a troopship, was decidedly out of sympathy with the military life. He had been, he thought, badly used by the army, which had steadfastly refused to recognize his qualities and the contribution he could make to the war effort. That is, he had not been given a command. It is hard to believe that this was a mistake: from Waugh's own account as well as from the recollections of his associates, he had an unerring instinct for the unforgivable, and both superiors and peers were consistently infuriated by his arrogance. In *Put Out More Flags*, however, Waugh has the last word.

The professional military man takes a variety of forms in the novel—the lieutenant-colonel of the bombardiers whom Basil approaches for a commission; Captain Mayfield of Alastair's company, who chooses his officer candidates by considering who contributes least to the company; the unnamed forces who send orders to three different groups to embark on the same ship at the same time; and the War Office as represented by Colonel Plum.

It is not just that war is mad, in Waugh's vision; it is that the military mind is closed, its intelligence is questionable, its motives are suspect, and its reputed efficiency is nonexistent. There are no institutional decencies in this world. The permissiveness of the modern world has destroyed it all. Everything, as Cedric Lyne realizes in the moment before his death, depends upon the individual in a world that constantly pushes one toward the group: "No one had anything against the individual; as long as he was alone he was free and safe; there's danger in numbers; divided we stand, united we fall, thought Cedric, striding happily towards the enemy, shaking from his boots the frustration of corporate life."

Cedric's death quickly dispels any illusion one may have about the primacy of reason in the modern world. His analyis is cogent; it makes sense; it simply fails to take into consideration the random nature of the world. That is, he may be right, but a spent bullet, ricocheting about the rocks, kills him anyway.

The houses of *Put Out More Flags* provide some of the best clues to the development of Waugh's attitudes in the novel and are helpful in understanding the values implicit in the work. Malfrey, country home of Basil's sister Barbara and her "prosaic and slightly absurd husband" Freddy, is openly sexual—Waugh describes it as "female and voluptuous," "spread out, sumptuously at ease, splendid, defenceless and provocative." That Malfrey is to be identified with England is clear in Barbara's perception that Hitler "was plotting the destruction of her home." Indeed, as the novel progresses, the direction of the war in Europe is reflected in Malfrey. As nations are invaded and fall, rooms are closed and shut off, and soon Barbara is living in "the little octagonal parlour which opened on the parterre." Even later she is driven to the orangery to keep warm.

The greatest threat to Malfrey, however, is not Herr Hitler; the greatest threat is domestic in origin—it is the Connollies. The Connollies, that family of egregious evacuees from Birmingham, are the scourge of the English countryside. The contrast between the classical beauty of Malfrey and the barbaric chaos with which the Connollies threaten it is clear in Waugh's description of Basil's encounter with the eldest Connolly on the first morning:

The corridor, though it was one of the by-ways of the house, had a sumptuous cornice and a high, coved ceiling; the door cases were enriched with classic pediments in whose broken entablatures stood busts of philosophers and composers. Other busts stood at regular intervals on marble pedestals. Everything in Malfrey was splendid and harmonious; everything except Doris, who, that morning, lurked in their path rubbing herself on a pilaster like a cow on a stump.

It is, ironically, the sexuality of Malfrey that defends it from the depredations of the lower classes, for Doris immediately falls for Basil with a fervor that lets him exploit her most effectively. It is not until he meets Mr. Todhunter ("death-hunter" in German) that a force stronger than sexual attraction enters the calculations.

In contrast to Malfrey, the houses the Connollies are allowed to savage are casual and eclectic in design and decoration. The Old Mill, home of the Harknesses, is self-consciously artistic, from the rush mats and bright Balkan rugs to the "tables and chairs of raw-looking beech." Like their house, the Harknesses lack internal harmony and repose, and are quickly reduced to a state of savagery by the depredations of the Connollies.

Certainly, although Waugh has his fun with the affected and artsy Harknesses, there is no real moral differences between them and the inhabitants of Malfrey. The real carriers of the moral superiority of Malfrey are the architecture and the furnishings.

The second large house in *Put Out More Flags* is the one Basil calls "Cedric's Folly." It is a "symmetrical, rectangular building" and, although we know little of the interior decoration, Cedric's disapproval of "David Lennox's grisailles," with their suggestion of modernism, is somehow reassuring. Cedric's house, too, suffers from the intrusions of the modern age, for it has been turned into a hospital, "given over to empty wards and an idle hospital staff." When Cedric returns home for his embarkation leave, he must stay at the farmhouse: he has been driven out of his home by the modern age in the form of war just as he was driven out of his marriage by the modern age in the form of Basil Seal.

The singular quality of the Lyne estate is its grottoes. It was, Cedric recalls, chiefly for the water that he and Angela bought the house, and it is chiefly for the grottoes that he loves it now. In the year in which Angela began her liaison with Basil, Cedric built a Chinese bridge over the water. Although the notion that water suggests life is not very fully developed in the novel, surely the identification of the water motif with the beginning of the Lynes' marriage is sufficient to establish the connection. The connection of the grottoes with the death of their marriage is more explicit: "Below in the hillside lay the cave which Cedric had bought the summer that Angela had refused to come with him to Salzburg; the summer when she met Basil." Thus connected to the caves and to death, Cedric Lyne is a marked man long before a bullet finds him in the little battlefield between his battalion headquarters and A Company.

Further illustrative of the fate of England are the London residence of Margot Metroland and the building housing the Ministry of Information. Something of the old world ends in *Put Out More Flags* when Margot closes her house and moves to the Ritz, as Waugh explains, "for ever," for while she is living at the Ritz, Curzon Street is bombed and the house is destroyed. It is hard to imagine a more effective image for establishing the fact that there will be no turning back, no return to prewar England for these denizens of the decades between the two wars.

Although Malfrey may be overrun by the yeomanry and Cedric's Folly may never quite recover from its stint as a hospital, one edifice reflects more clearly than any other the world to come. It is the Ministry of Information, a "gross mass of masonry," "insulting the autumnal sky" and it is part of London University. As the beauty of Malfrey and Cedric's Folly suggest the values of an England past, the execrable appearance, interior and exterior, of the Ministry of Information displays the faults of England present.

Not only has the building a bland and boring facade, inside it is utterly dismal and depressing in decor. Mr. Bentley's office is a disused chemistry laboratory with a white porcelain sink into which the tap drips "monotonously." Neither Mr. Bentley's sculpture portraits by Nollekens nor the mahogany prie-dieu of the Church of England advisor can assuage the architectural sins of the Ministry of Information.

4

The Moral Center

In the three novels he wrote as the war wound down and the world settled into uneasy peace, Waugh came to grips with the theme at the center of his moral universe—the centrality of the Christian faith in the life of modern man. Although they are similar thematically, however, the novels are distinct from one another stylistically. *Brideshead Revisited* is a lush, romantic, melodramatic first-person narrative. *The Loved One* is a compact, terse satire on modern culture. And *Helena* is a historical novel based on the life of a saint. Despite the diversity of forms, these three novels represent the stage in Waugh's development in which he discovered a new voice and a new meaning in his vocation as a writer.

In *Brideshead Revisited* and *Helena*, Waugh moves away from the steadfastly external, Firbankian type of writer who wants to exploit the absurdities of surfaces, leaving the depths to his readers. Instead, he develops a greater sense of engagement with his characters, their feelings, and their motives. In *The Loved One* the style more nearly approximates his earlier allusive approach. But the books are linked by the centrality of the Christian experience.

As the styles differ, so do the rhetorical strategies employed. For example, in *Brideshead Revisited* and *Helena*, Waugh uses positive instruction by showing the Christian faith at work in the world and in the lives of his characters. In *The Loved One* he employs the satirist's strategy of negative instruction. The meaninglessness of the lives of the Southern Californians serves to illustrate the grotesquerie of a people who want the comforts of religious forms without having to be bothered to believe in them.

Brideshead Revisited

Like *A Handful of Dust*, *Brideshead Revisited* now exists in more than one version. In its original form (published in 1945) the novel was "an attempt to trace the workings of the divine purpose in a pagan world, in the lives of an English Catholic family, half-paganized themselves, in the world of 1923-39." One hears the voice Waugh discovered in "Work Suspended" in this novel. Although the staccato lines of conversation are not absent from *Brideshead*, the first-person narrator gives the book a focal point that the earlier novels never had. Charles Ryder may not be correct in his assessments throughout the novel, but we know him and his character, and we must measure his interpretations against the evidence we see through his eyes. The presence of such an intermediary between ourselves and experience creates the impression of a moral center in the novel that the earlier works lacked.

With *Brideshead Revisited*, Waugh's work took a dramatically different direction, and one that was not happily received by those who loved his early style. The *Times Literary Supplement* found that although the book was "often extremely amusing," it was flawed because "nowhere in the book does the humour stand alone, nowhere does it suggest any sort of detachment or disinterestedness of mind." He concluded that "Mr. Waugh has his felicities of illustration and phrase, of course, but seems in general to have had his style cramped by a too obviously preconceived idea."[1] Henry Reed, writing for the *New Statesman*, had some serious reservations but allowed that "underneath all the disfigurements, and never for long out of sight, there is in *Brideshead Revisited* a fine and brilliant book; its plan and a good deal of its execution are masterly."[2] The *Spectator* was less grudging with its admiration, saying that the novel was Waugh's "most ambitious . . . and his best." The reviewer particularly praised the creation of characters, saying, "Anything improbable, anything unreasonable, would have been disastrous. It is the measure of Evelyn Waugh's success that every move in the untwisting of this tangle appears not merely probable but pre-ordained. . . . Much seems to surprise: yet all is prepared."[3]

Waugh was concerned from the beginning that *Brideshead Revisited* would not be understood or appreciated in the United States. For the most part, this fear was unfounded: the novel was reviewed well by the *New York Times Book Review* where it was declared to have "the depth and weight that are found in a writer working in his prime, in the full powers of an eager, good mind and a skilled hand, retaining the best of what he has already learned,"[4] and the Book-of-the-Month-Club selected it. On the other hand, Edmund Wilson, writing in the *New Yorker*, found *Brideshead Revisited* to be "a bitter blow" and excoriated Waugh for his lack of common sense, his banality, his snobbery, and his deteriorating style.[5]

The plot of *Brideshead Revisited* is quite straightforward. Charles Ryder, introduced in the prologue, is an infantry captain, a painter, and a divorced man. When he and his company arrive at the grounds of Brideshead, a large country house in Wiltshire, Charles is reminded of his earlier associations with the house and the family who owned it.

Book 1 is entitled "Et In Arcadia Ego," ("I, too, was in Arcadia"). This wonderfully ambiguous line, which traditionally appears on tombs and in paintings of tombs, can mean either "I (a person) was also in a happy and bucolic country" or "I (a tomb and thus death) was also in Arcadia." If it means the latter, then the implication is that even when people are happiest, death is among them. The ambiguity suggests to the reader that the idyllic happiness of the opening scenes will not last.

In book 1, Charles recalls his friendship with Sebastian Flyte, a beautiful, sensitive, and driven younger son of an English Catholic family with whom he attended Oxford. The first part of the section is devoted to the university life of the two young men. They give luncheons, drink amazing quantities of wine, entertain one another over the long vacations, first at Brideshead and later in Venice. In their second Oxford year, the two attend a party in London after which Sebastian is arrested for driving while drunk. This misadventure brings them under the supervision of Mr. Samgrass, a fellow of All Souls College. In the process, Sebastian's family are introduced, one by one.

The elder brother is Brideshead, called Bridey. He is serious, pious, and absolutely unable to take any perspective but a Catholic one. He is the head of the house in England in his father's absence. Cordelia, the younger sister, is vivacious, direct, and has an unwavering faith. She dotes on Sebastian and hopes she has a calling to join a religious order. Julia, who resembles Sebastian, is beautiful and restless and does not think much about religion. She wants to marry well and regards her Catholicism, if at all, as a hindrance to that end.

Lord Marchmain, Sebastian's father, lives in Venice with his companion of many years, Cara. He, too, has fallen away from his religion. Sebastian's mother, who is the center of the family, is absolutely firm in her faith. She is a saintly woman who sees her son following a self-destructive course and tries to stop him. In trying to stop him, she drives him to greater excesses.

When Sebastian's drinking becomes obsessive, his family removes him from Oxford and sends him abroad, first with the odious Mr. Samgrass and later with the competent Rex Mottram, a vulgar colonial turned politician who later marries Julia. Both times Sebastian gives his chaperon the slip. He finally ends up in Morocco, living with a young German named Kurt who is willing to let Sebastian take care of him.

When Sebastian is removed from Oxford, Charles also leaves, to attend an art school in France. He returns to London during the general strike of 1926 to find Lady Marchmain dying and the family concerned that Sebastian should know. So Charles travels to Fez to find Sebastian who is, by now, thoroughly alcoholic, ill, and unable to travel, but quite happy having someone rely upon him.

In book 2, "A Twitch upon the Thread," Sebastian drops out of sight, and Julia and Charles become the center of the action. In the years following Lady Marchmain's death, Charles becomes a successful architectural painter. He marries Celia Mulcaster, the sister of a college acquaintance, and has two children. Returning home from a two year painting tour of Latin America, Charles meets Julia on board ship, and they become lovers.

Charles spends the best part of two years with Julia at Brideshead. When brother Brideshead comes home to announce his impending marriage and informs Julia that his intended wife cannot come into the house in which Charles and Julia are "living in sin," however, their liaison begins to unravel.

Celia divorces Charles and Julia divorces Rex; Charles and Julia intend to marry. Cordelia returns with news of Sebastian who has become a hanger-on at a religious house in Morocco. He has found his way back to the church. Then Lord Marchmain announces his intention to return to Brideshead—he wants to come home to die. Despite Charles's hopes, Lord Marchmain repents at the end and accepts absolution. His deathbed repentance shows Julia her duty, and she leaves Charles.

Finally, although Charles is bereft of all those things which might have been thought to recall him from exile (a family, a creative profession, a popular war), it is only the church and his sense of the unity of the faith that can make him feel at peace with himself. For the first time Waugh can be seen to understand and, indeed, to argue that secular commitments, whether public or private, cannot make modern man feel at home in the world. He discovers that the solution to the exile problem that has vexed him for his entire literary life can only be resolved in a religious context. In *Brideshead Revisited*, however, Waugh only brought his hero to an understanding of the problem and an awareness of a possible solution. He still had not attempted to depict the events of a life lived in the household of the faith. For such a project Waugh's readers had to wait for the war trilogy and the life of Guy Crouchback.

The "epilogue" reveals that Lord Marchmain has given Brideshead Castle to Julia, that Julia and Cordelia are abroad doing war work, and that Charles has converted to Catholicism. And that he is happy.

Brideshead Castle itself is very much at the center of the novel. It is called a "castle," Sebastian explains, because it used to be one. The present house was built "in Inigo Jones's time" (the seventeenth century) of the stones from an earlier structure that actually was a castle. It is an old structure, then, reconstructed from the materials of another, much older. It lies enclosed in a valley near the headwaters of a river called the Bride, amid woods "planted a century and a half ago so that about this date, it might be seen in its maturity." Thus the house is a perfect symbol of the English Catholic Church, which was also established long ago and, for Waugh, was just reaching its period of greatest importance. The identification is reinforced by the name, for the church is often described as the bride of Christ.

The house is large and baroque, decorated architecturally with elaborate and intricate forms and designs. The fireplaces are not just marble, but sculptured marble; the coved ceilings are not only coved, but frescoed with pictures of gods and heroes; the mirrors are gilt and the fountain in the terrace is a wonder of "daring and invention," with its "fantastic tropical animals" and its "Egyptian obelisk of red sandstone."

For Charles, whose tastes have been, as he tells us, puritan, the richness and liveliness of the architecture of Brideshead makes the house itself seem to be a source of life. He is particularly drawn to the ornate and bubbling fountain, which becomes a central image of the novel, tracing the progress of the pagan/humanistic values Charles brings to this world. The physical beauty that is so important a part of the way Waugh describes the charm of the Flytes and the love they inspire in Charles is mirrored in Waugh's treatment of the fountain. As Charles's role in the world changes, the fountain changes to express the change.

First, the fountain is a central part of the idyllic long vacation in which Charles and Sebastian are perfectly happy:

And we would leave the golden candlelight of the dining-room for the starlight outside and sit on the edge of the fountain, cooling our hands in the water and listening drunkenly to its splash and gurgle over the rocks.

In the early days of Charles's and Julia's love, the fountain is likewise a source of solace, although rather than the coolness of his youthful love for Sebastian, the fountain now reflects the passionate intensity of Charles's love for Julia:

There Julia sat, in a tight little gold tunic and a white gown, one hand in the water idly turning an emerald ring to catch the fire of the sunset; the carved animals mounted over her dark head in a cumulus of green moss and glowing stone and dense shadow, and the waters round them flashed and bubbled and broke into scattered beads of flame.

Those "scattered beads of flame" signal clearly the physical intensity of the relationship between the two lovers.

When Bridey returns home to inform Julia and Charles of his intention to marry and to take up occupancy of Brideshead Castle, Julia's semihysterical monologue on the subject of sin also takes place at the side of the fountain. All the color and light has vanished from the fountain in this scene: Julia is simply a "white skirt against the stones," and minutes later Charles finds her sitting "in the darkest refuge, on a wooden seat, in a bay of the clipped box which encircled the basin." There she recognizes for the first time that the values that had seemed to offer comfort and refreshment, the worldliness implied in the fountain, had instead left her desolate in the black-and-white world of sin.

In its final scene, the fountain is empty of water (i.e., dead). It has been fenced to keep mankind out and in response the soldiers have treated it as a trash receptacle: "all the drivers throw their cigarette-ends and the remains of the sandwiches there, and you can't get to it to clean it up." Not only does the fountain no longer offer comfort and refreshment, it has become, among this race of brutish men, an eyesore and a symbol of the modern wasteland.

Much the same is true of the progress of Brideshead Castle as a whole. The walls and fireplaces have been covered, but even that effort has not prevented the despoiling of the office, Lady Marchmain's parlor, and the tapestry hall. Nor has good sense protected the serenity of the view from the terrace from the enroachments of latrines and an auxiliary road. The modern age, which Charles calls "the age of Hooper," has thoroughly overrun the last vestiges of gentleness, honor, and beauty.

While the house and the fountain reflect the progress of humanistic values in the world of the novel, the chapel reflects Charles's spiritual progress and the religious values in his world. The chapel, built by Lord Marchmain for his wife, is the newest part of Brideshead Castle. Like the rest of the house, it is built from old stones and thus shares the long tradition Brideshead represents.

The chapel is, as Sebastian says when it is first introduced, "a monument of art nouveau" and Waugh's description of it catches for the reader the richness and linearity of that movement at the end of the nineteenth century as well as its typical symbolic themes:

> Angels in printed cotton smocks, rambler-roses, flower-spangled meadows, frisking lambs, texts in Celtic script, saints in armour, covered the walls in an intricate pattern of clear, bright colours. There was a triptych of pale oak, carved so as to give it the peculiar property

of seeming to have been moulded in plasticine. The sanctuary lamp and all the metal furniture were of bronze, hand-beaten to the patina of a pockmarked skin; the altar steps had a carpet of grass-green, strewn with white and gold daisies.

Although the chapel is consistent and unified aesthetically, Charles is appalled by it. The nicest thing he can say in reply to Bridey's direct question about its artistic merit is, "I think it's a remarkable example of its period. Probably in eighty years it will be greatly admired." In his youthful arrogance and his worldly state, he can appreciate it only as it exists in a certain period and in aesthetic terms. As a religious structure, it has no meaning at all for him, and because *Brideshead Revisited* is his book, Cordelia's "I think it's *beautiful*" appears to be a revelation of her sentimentality and naïveté at this early stage.

When the chapel at Brideshead Castle is closed after the death of Lady Marchmain, Cordelia's observation that "suddenly, there wasn't any chapel there any more, just an oddly decorated room" calls attention to the importance of the unseen spirit of God in the meaning of the chapel. Clearly it is not the decoration of the chapel or even its origin in the old stone of the castle which preceded it that justifies Waugh's giving that "oddly decorated room" its powerful position as the last image of the work.

When Charles enters the chapel at the close of the novel, he notes that it has not changed: "the art-nouveau paint was as fresh and bright as ever; the art-nouveau lamp burned once more before the altar." But the fact that the decoration of the chapel is unchanged is really insignificant. What is significant is not the decor but the flame, "a small red flame—a beaten-copper lamp of deplorable design, relit before the beaten-copper doors of a tabernacle," which comes to symbolize faith. It is faith, not art, that assumes different forms through the years and still continues unchanged.

In making Brideshead Castle the central image of the novel,

Waugh for the first time employs the symbol of a building without being ironic. In *Decline and Fall* he had presented the creation of Llanabba Castle as economic exploitation and a failure to recognize the spirit of existing architecture; in *A Handful of Dust* the chromium plating of the small parlor at Hetton Abbey was another of the assaults of the savages on Gothic man; but the rebuilding of Brideshead is a positive act.

A love of architecture and an interest in building is central to Charles's sensibility. In his youth, he reports, his taste was for structures far less various and far more restrained than Brideshead, but he comes to love the infinite variety and richness of the house that used to be a castle. Almost the only room in which Charles can find nothing to be aesthetically admired is the chapel.

For Sebastian, the date of construction of Brideshead is irrelevant: "What does it matter when it was built, if it's pretty?" he asks. For Charles, however, who longs to understand his world logically, the origins matter. At Brideshead, he learns from Sebastian to rely upon something beyond the world of five senses and three dimensions, but he does not quite know what that something is. He thinks it is love—his love for Sebastian and the Marchmain family and their love for him. In his innocence and adolescent egocentricity, he imagines that the building and rebuilding of Brideshead and the designing and redesigning of the grounds have all been aimed at this moment, his moment of intense personal happiness: "All this had been planned and planted a century and a half ago so that, at about this date, it might be seen in its maturity."

When Charles returns to Brideshead during the war and sees it desolate, the experience reaffirms his sense of exclusion. What had appeared to be paradise was not. The building and landscaping had not tended toward perfect unity and beauty to validate his happiness but toward desolation and decay to validate his loneliness:

The builders did not know the uses to which their work would descend; they made a new house with the stones of the old castle; year by year, generation after generation, they enriched and extended it; year by year the great harvest of timber in the park grew to ripeness; until in sudden frost, came the age of Hooper; the place was desolate and the work all brought to nothing; *Quomodo sedet sola civitas.* Vanity of vanities, all is vanity.

This pose, too, is somewhat ego-centered, but it is in the nature of a romantic sensibility to insist that one's own concerns and cares are reflected in the world. Further, Charles is never quite required to give up his egocentric ways. He does discover the thread of continuity throughout the ages, tending toward his happiness, but he finds it not in the house and the delights of the world of three dimensions and five senses nor in the love of Sebastian and Julia of which the house reminds him. Rather, he finds it in the flame from the lamp of deplorable design and its reminder of God's love.

What is odd about the building in this book is that Charles (and every other reasonable character) deplores the destruction of the beautiful English homes that are immortalized in *Ryder's Country Seats.* So on the one hand the reader rightfully deplores the effect of the modern age on the beauty and traditional values of the English upper classes. At the same time, the reader must be aware that misplaced trust in that beauty and those values will lead to disillusionment. This fact is illustrated over and over with Charles, Sebastian, and Julia. The reader must recognize, as these characters come to do, that the values of the society that has disappeared under the assault of the modern age, admirable though they may be, are inessential.

The buildings are important to Charles and to the people who hire him because they represent the closest thing to God he knows—that moment of inspiration that makes the whole greater than the sum of the parts. And, the book argues, that is what faith does for people—it makes them more nearly whole. This is the significance of the repeated references to Rex Mottram and Charles as being missing some important piece or as being "a tiny bit of a man pretending to be the whole." When Charles and Rex are both outside the faith, the differences between them are less of kind than of degree; without faith they are both incomplete.

Like the heroes who have preceded him, Charles is an exile. His mother is dead and his father's attitude toward him varies from sublime indifference to obvious antagonism. Charles is unwelcome in his father's house and perhaps, judging by the eagerness with which his father agrees to send him to Paris to attend an art school, also in his father's country. After his first year at Oxford, he drops all of his university friends except Sebastian, so when Sebastian is sent away, he is desolate. His marriage to Celia fails to make him feel that he is part of a whole at the best of times, and when he discovers that she has been unfaithful to him, his sense of separateness is exacerbated. Thus the themes of exile, loneliness, and isolation are central to the novel.

The exile theme is most intricately worked out in the image of the deserted city that Waugh evokes at three points in the novel with increasing symbolic richness. *Quomodo sedet sola civitas* (How the city sits, solitary) is introduced by Cordelia when she tells Charles how the chapel was closed after Lady Marchmain's death:

> "You've never been to Tenebrae I suppose?"
> "Never."
> "Well, if you had you'd know what the Jews felt about their temple. *Quomodo sedet sola civitas.* . . it's a beautiful chant."

The theme reappears on the ocean liner as Charles returns from Latin America and contemplates the emptiness of the life he is about to resume: "Here, where wealth is no longer gorgeous and power has no dignity." And it appears for the last time at the end of the novel as Charles surveys the desolation of Brideshead and thinks, "Vanity of vanities, all is vanity."

Quomodo sedet sola civitas is the first line of "The Lamentations of Jeremiah" and refers to the devastation of Jerusalem; however, it has traditionally been read by Christians as prefiguring the death of Christ, which explains why it has become a part of the Tenebrae service on the Wednesday of Holy Week. In using the line in a way that shows Charles first being concerned with the material world (the chapel itself), then being concerned with the values of the material world (the values of prewar England), but ultimately being concerned with the Christian context, Waugh is following the traditional Catholic reading of the passage.

When Cordelia first introduces the notion of the empty city, she makes the connection between the city and Christ, saying that in closing the chapel, removing the altar stone and blowing out the lamp, the priest had made it seem "as though from now on it was always to be Good Friday." Charles, at this stage a "poor agnostic," cannot make the connection. The closest he can come to understanding the pull of the faith is to liken it to love, for his love for Sebastian and the Marchmain family has been the strongest force in his young life.

In resisting the sense that the devastation of the city means loss of love, Charles devotes himself to painting, an activity in which he sometimes, though not often, experiences the sense of oneness and completion he had felt during his friendship with Sebastian. However, as his career progresses, he finds that he cannot depend upon art and the material world to provide this transcendence. His explanation is material as his refuge had been—"Wealth is no longer gorgeous and power has no dignity." That is, the world is deteriorating and its degradation explains the lack of the sense of transcendence.

When Julia appears and Charles falls in love with her, he feels that he has recaptured the joy and hence the transcendence he experienced with Sebastian, who now seems to be a forerunner of his love for Julia. However, the parallel is closer than he knows, for human love is no more the answer here than it was earlier. Although it is temporarily a way to oneness, it can no more be constant and unchanging than the world can.

When Charles returns to Brideshead as an army officer, he has lost all earthly paths to the sense of oneness he seeks—Sebastian and Julia are beyond his reach, artistic creation no longer seems possible, the material world continues to deteriorate and cannot give pleasure, and he feels utterly estranged from everything around him—men, mores, even the military. At last the city seems to be foresaken in every sense. Only then can Charles, recently converted (saying, "ancient words newly learned" in the chapel), perceive that the one constant source of the feeling of unity and transcendence he seeks is faith, symbolized by "a small red flame . . . burning anew among the old stones."

The Loved One

When an invitation from MGM to adapt *Brideshead Revisited* for the screen resulted in a trip to Los Angeles for him and his wife, Waugh was as fascinated by the savagery of this new jungle as he had been by the Brazilian river valley of *A Handful of Dust*. He was particularly taken by the appalling commercializing of death and the accompanying euphemisms he discovered at Forest Lawn Cemetery. His gleeful disgust with the savage rites of the North Americans led to the masterful short novel *The Loved One*.

The Loved One was an instant success on both sides of the Atlantic. Cyril Connolly, introducing the novel to the readers of *Horizon*, wrote, "It is, in my opinion, one of the most perfect short novels of the last ten years and the most complete of Waugh's creations."[6] The *New Republic*, agreed: "As a piece of writing it is nearly faultless; as satire it is an act of devastation, an angry, important, moral effort that does not fail."[7] The *Times Literary Supplement* called it Waugh's "most mature and most awe-inspiring satire . . . a short piece of coruscating brilliance."[8]

In a letter to Connolly preceding the publication of *The Loved One* in *Horizon*, Waugh wrote:

The ideas I had in mind in writing were: 1st & quite predominantly overexcitement with the scene of Forest Lawn. 2nd the Anglo-American impasse—never the twain shall meet, 3rd there is no such thing as an American. They are all exiles, uprooted, transplanted & doomed to sterility. The ancestral gods they have abjured get them in the end. I tried to indicate this in Aimee's last hours. 4th the European raiders who come for the spoils & if they are lucky make for home with them. 5th Memento mori, old style, not specifically Californian.[9]

The plot of *The Loved One* turns on the adventures of Dennis Barlow, an ex-airman and poet, who has left England for the milder climes of Hollywood and a term as a scriptwriter at the Megalopolitan film studios. Encouraged by Sir Francis Hinsley, an English man of letters who has been devoured by the studio system and rejected as a failure, Dennis leaves the movie business and, determined to return to poetry, takes a job at The Happier Hunting Ground, a pet cemetery, much to the distress of the English expatriates in the city.

When Sir Francis is fired by Megalopolitan Pictures and commits suicide, Dennis is commissioned by the English community to arrange a suitable funeral at Whispering Glades, where death is never mentioned and the dead are called "the loved ones." There, among debased traces of western culture, he finds Aimee Thanatogenos, and recognizes her as a true decadent, intrinsically different from the uniform, standard, hygienic, plastic, predictable American women around her.

Aimee, whose names mean "beloved bringer of death," is a cosmetician at Whispering Glades. She is in love with Mr. Joyboy, the chief embalmer. She is also "half in love with easeful death."

Poorly educated and impressionable, Aimee is much taken with the young English poet; Dennis, for his part, is intrigued by Whispering Glades and its decadent servant. Because she loves poetry but knows none of the classics, Dennis courts Aimee by sending her copies of some of the greatest lyrics in English, allowing her to assume that they are his own compositions.

When Aimee discovers that Dennis works at The Happier Hunting Ground (which desecrates the image of Whispering Glades by imitating it in some ways) and that he is not the author of the poems he has sent, she is furious and expresses her intention to break her engagement to Dennis and return to Mr. Joyboy. Dennis, however, refuses to release her from her vow of constancy, and the newspaper columnist who writes advice to the lovelorn loses patience and advises her to jump off a tall building. Instead, she commits suicide in Mr. Joyboy's embalming room.

Terrified that his career will be ruined by the scandal, Mr. Joyboy goes to Dennis for help. Dennis solves the problem by cremating his "Loved One" in the furnace of The Happier Hunting Ground. He departs for England, taking with him "a great, shapeless chunk of experience, the artist's load" and leaving for Mr. Joyboy a yearly postcard that reads, "Your little Aimee is wagging her tail in heaven tonight, thinking of you."

Coming as it does after *Brideshead Revisited* and the explicit treatment in that novel of the tension between secular and religious values, *The Loved One* may at first appear to be among the most secular of Waugh's works. In fact, however, a religious enthusiasm informs the entire novel. It is the absence of a genuine religious impulse, the tendency to think of religion as a business rather than as an expression of the order of the world, that accounts for the spiritual sterility and, ultimately, the spiritual death characteristic of Waugh's fictional California.

Pagan religions abound in this version of the wasteland. Sir Francis searches Celtic mythology for the new incarnation of Juanita del Pablo; Aimee is a nautch girl (an Indian ceremonial dancer) and a vestal virgin at one time and a descendant of worshipers of ancient Greek gods at another. Of Orthodox Christianity, however, there is little. Of charity, the cutthroat world of Hollywood can offer even less. When Sir Francis can create a product that will sell, he is valuable. When he cannot, he is no longer considered to be human. The successful and the unsuccessful are of different orders of being. Of hope, there is less than charity, except in the basest sense. The city is a spiritual wasteland, from which not even death provides an escape. The recurrence of the suicide motif (Sir Francis and then Aimee) is ample illustration of the failure of the secular to provide hope. And in this culture, Christianity is represented only by nonsectarian clergymen who, like the modern churchmen of *Decline and Fall*, seem not to be required to believe anything. It is the absence of faith, of course, that accounts for the lack of hope and charity in this lost land between the mountains and the sea.

The theme of the exile is clearly central to *The Loved One*. For the English community, Hollywood is another scarcely civilized outpost of the empire, where preservation of the forms is essential. It is the attention to English conventions of dress and behavior that prevents them from "going native," that is, from picking up American habits and behaviors. They drink their whisky and soda, read *Horizon* (the magazine in which English readers first met this novel), and wear their old school ties. They even have a cricket club. But their treasured "Englishness" is strictly a matter of surfaces. In important matters, for example spiritual matters, they are as hopeless as the natives.

For Sir Francis Hinsley, the exile is threefold. He lives in a new and savage land, far from home; he has outlived the intellectual milieu in which he was comfortable, and he is a failure, which also sets him apart from the rest of the English community and, later, from all living souls. In fact, Sir Francis's plight illustrates the essential isolation of all the inhabitants of Hollywood.

As Waugh observed in his letter to Connolly, Americans

too are all exiles. There is no such thing as a native Californian in the novel, although it is nonetheless possible to "go native." The sense of isolation Waugh wants to create is an integral part of the character of Aimee. Like so many Waugh characters, she is, for all practical purposes, an orphan. Her father, who "lost his money in religion," left her mother and the area. Aimee's mother then "went East to look for him . . . and died there." She explains her reason for moving to Whispering Glades by saying, "I was just glad to serve people that couldn't talk."

For Aimee, as later for Pinfold, the line dividing exile and withdrawal is faint. As a servant of death, she is set apart from the others, and she shares in the general American exile. But it is the secular nature of Whispering Glades that exacerbates her outsideness; if she were part of the sort of religious society for which Waugh longed, the sort that makes one part of "the communion of the saints," her sense of exile would be ameliorated. The essence of the California of *The Loved One*, however, is form over content, so she can have no sense of the traditions that could give meaning to her life or content to her empty forms. She is cut off from any system into which she can withdraw. For her there are no catacombs; when she rejects the world, nothing else remains.

Dennis, on the other hand, is only a physical exile. As an artist, he is in touch with the traditions of his literary world; similarly, as an explorer from the old world, he is aware of the traditions of civilization. His protection is his status as a traveler, a "frontiersman," a gatherer of material. Although he is in California, he never becomes a Californian; that is, he never adopts the attitudes and mentality that could mean he cannot go home. In this he differs from the English expatriates like Sir Francis Hinsley and Ambrose Abercrombie who have been so seduced by the spirit of Hollywood that they have "gone native" inwardly, though not, perhaps, outwardly.

Waugh also uses description of landscape, or at least certain epithets applied to landscape to enhance the sense of exile. When, in the opening paragraphs, we find "native huts," a "plot of weeds between the veranda and the dry water-hole," and a reference to Englishmen "exiled in the barbarous regions of the world," we anticipate a geographically isolated location for the tale. In fact, however, as the language suggests, the isolation is spiritual and psychological rather than physical. This conclusion is confirmed by the response Waugh attributes to Dennis when he finds himself in thrall to Whispering Glades: "In a zone of insecurity in the mind where none but the artist dare trespass, the tribes were mustering. Dennis, the frontier-man, could read the signs."

When the native huts are revealed to be bungalows and the dry waterhole a swimming pool, the reader recognizes that this is a world of spiritual and psychological isolation, rather than one of physical isolation. Other examples of Waugh's use of the physical to suggest the spiritual and psychological distances between people abound: Mr. Joyboy lives "a long way down Santa Monica Boulevard" in a housing development where many of the lots are vacant. The first poem Dennis reads in the novel is Tennyson's "Tithonus," which is about a beautiful young man who is cut off from humanity by being given eternal life but not eternal youth. The line Dennis takes as his mantra is "Here at the quiet limit of the world." Aimee lives in a "concrete cell which she called her apartment." And Dennis observes to Mr. Joyboy that "no one in Southern California . . . ever inquires what goes on beyond the mountains."

The generalization one can make about the Southern California of *The Loved One* is that everything is the opposite of what it seems. The civilization is so thoroughly debased that every value has been turned on its head. People talk, but "nothing they say is designed to be heard," as Sir Francis points out. Food is served, but it is not intended to be tasted—whether nutburgers ("It is not so much their nastiness as their total absence of taste that shocks one"), or Kaiser's Stoneless Peaches ("Dennis recalled that he had once tried to eat one of Mr. Kaiser's much-advertised products and had discovered a ball of damp, sweet cotton-wool"). And Whispering Glades, through which humanity ought to pass on its way out of this world and in to the next, keeps its eye firmly fixed on the mundane and the transitory. Flowers, for example, are allowed in the cemetery because they are living and remind one of life, unless, of course, they are arranged in the shape of a cross. A cross is not allowed because it is not "natural" and because it reminds one of death.

The various zones of the park are committed to the pursuit of earthly delights: the Lover's Nest is characterized by "a very beautiful marble replica of Rodin's famous statue, the Kiss"; the Lake Isle, a favorite trysting place, is decorated with artificial bee hives (and artificial buzz); and the Lover's Nook features a Robert Burns poem that talks about love that lasts as long as life ("while the sands o life shall run") but omits the allusion to death with which the poem ends.

In the name of celebrating the "natural," the Dreamer and his staff perpetrate the most appalling assaults on the dead and on the survivors. In the interest of having the dead look "life-like," Mr. Joyboy arranges their features in one of several available "natural expressions." When he begins to court Aimee, he sends her corpse after corpse whose features have been manipulated into an absolutely inappropriate "Radiant Childhood smile." In addition, the unfortunate dead are painted for their appearance in the "Slumber Room" in colors that are obviously overdone but that theoretically will appear natural in the subdued light of the viewing room.

As Dennis discovers, however, the "natural" for which Whispering Glades strives is far more artificial and hence more disgusting than the bloody tooth and claw of authentic nature can be. When Aimee has finished with Sir Francis, Dennis looks at the body of his friend: "the face was entirely horrible; as ageless as a tortoise and as inhuman; a painted and smirking obscene travesty by comparison with which the devil-mask Dennis had found in the noose was a festive adornment."

Finally, the buildings of Whispering Glades illustrate the total confusion of the real and the artificial that reigns in this land. The University Church, for example, in which Sir Francis Hinsley's funeral service takes place, is identified in the recorded lecture not as the University Church but as the Church of St. Peter-without-the-walls. Not only does the Dreamer give the church one name and call it by another, but he willfully changes the meaning of the name by which it is called, so that "without-the-walls" (i.e., outside the walls) becomes *without walls* (i.e., having no walls). And that is not the end of the confusion. Having made the phrase mean "having no walls," he then gives the building walls "of glass and grade A steel." The chain of absurdity threatens to extend forever.

This confusion between what a thing is and what it is called is developed most delightfully in Waugh's treatment of the evolution of Juanita del Pablo. Originally called "Baby Aaronson," the woman is given a nose job and singing lessons and sent off to become another person. Sir Francis explains: "*I* named her. *I* made her an anti-Fascist refugee. *I* said she hated men because of her treatment by Franco's Moors."

The unnamed person originally called Baby Aaronson and then called Juanita del Pablo is about to be called by yet another name. Her case parallels the situation that occurred when Aimee's parents determined to change her name because of their disappointment with Aimee Semple McPherson's brand of religion: "Once you start changing a name, you see, there's no reason ever to stop. "Furthermore, Juanita's change of identity raises an interesting problem: If what a thing is changes when its name changes, can the thing be said to exist in any real way? The suggestion in Juanita's case is that she no longer exists; once the reality conferred upon her by language is removed, nothing remains.

The purpose of language in *The Loved One*, as the example of the various names of the University Church suggests, is not communication. In fact, a major theme is that the function of language is to avoid communication. Waugh is having so much fun developing devices by which his characters can fail to communicate, that he can scarcely bear to represent a straightforward conversation. The theme of the debasing of language and its implications for human communication is first introduced in Hinsley's observation that the denizens of Hollywood "talk entirely for their own pleasure. Nothing they say is designed to be heard." Should anyone go so far as to listen, it is difficult to tell what he would make of what he would hear. Waugh presents characters whose language is intended to distort rather than to represent experience.

For example, when Ambrose Abercrombie appears at Hinsley's bungalow, he chides Sir Francis for dropping out of sight: "You shouldn't hide yourself away, Frank, you old hermit." Yet the narrator reveals that Sir Francis has been in exactly the same house for twenty years, and that Sir Ambrose, who has been ignoring his old friend, is clearly off the mark in this jovial accusation.

In just the same way, the operators of the two cemeteries in the novel deal in euphemisms to avoid the reality of their functions. Dennis is less apt at this game than the unnamed mortuary hostess of Whispering Glades, as his first professional conversation shows:

> "Were you thinking of interment or incineration?"
> "Pardon me?"
> "Burned or buried?"

Such a clear translation of the jargon of the trade appears rarely if at all in the more-elevated society of Whispering Glades, although violent shifts in levels of diction are important in Waugh's arsenal of humorous techniques. Compare the performance of the mortuary hostess with Dennis's effort above: "Normal disposal is by inhumement, entombment, inurnment or immurement, but many people just lately prefer insarcophagusment."

This is an absolutely brilliant sentence—look at the way the rhythm and sound of the words "inhumement, entombment, inurnment or immurement" ripple along musically to be set off by the jaw-breaking difficulty of "insarcophagusment." And look at the distance in intelligibility between the proffered "inhumement" and Dennis's translation, "We want my friend buried."

So safe are the employees of Whispering Glades with their language that obfuscates rather than clarifies, that any information that does not fit their rather arbitrary definition of reality is simply transformed into a satisfactory form. Thus it is that agnosticism becomes a religion when the mortuary hostess inquires about Hinsley's beliefs:

> "Was your Loved One of any special religion?"
> "An Agnostic."
> "We have two non-sectarian churches in the Park and a number of non-sectarian pastors."

The exchange is similar when she asks about his race:

> "I presume the Loved One was Caucasian?"
> "No, why did you think that? He was purely English."
> "English are purely Caucasian, Mr. Barlow. This is a restricted park."

In using language to make experience less rather than more immediate, Waugh's characters do precisely the opposite of what the artist does. The poems to which Dennis returns again and again and with which he courts Aimee are classics of English literature because they have spoken to generations of readers in ways that made experience more, not less, accessible. Response to these poems is the only thing Aimee and Dennis have in common. Yet Aimee's language is so limited (and because her language is limited, her thoughts are as well), that she can only describe some of the greatest love poems in the English language as "unethical." She simply has no other way to think about physical passion. "A rich glint of lunacy" is right.

In Mr. Slump, the Guru Brahmin, Aimee finds a counselor who fails to communicate as well. He will not, and sometimes cannot, read and understand, and his responses are a matter of empty forms embodied in someone else's style. Furthermore, Aimee's final telephone call to him illustrates the ubiquity of Hinsley's precept that "nothing they say is designed to be heard." When Slump puts the telephone receiver down on the bar and lets Aimee talk until she runs out of things to say, he is giving perfect form to Waugh's idea that everyone under the California sun is completely isolated.

The scene in which Mr. Slump puts the receiver down on the bar is, of course, a repetition of an earlier scene in which Dennis does the same thing to a hysterical caller to The Happier Hunting Ground. The repetition links Aimee's death with the death of the Sealyham terrier that introduces Dennis's profession, and the linkage is completed when Aimee finds her way to the same crematorium and burns as Dennis sits in the office and reads. The only difference is that this time he reads a novel instead of poetry.

On nearly every page there are additional examples of the use of language to disguise or deny experience. Mom's insults are "little jokes" and her rudeness is "treating you natural." People don't die, they "pass over." Embalmers and cosmeticians are "artists" and drunks are "Gurus." So the exile theme, begun by the geographical allusions that establish the inhabitants of Southern California as exiles, is picked up in the language theme that shows how they are cut off not only from the world but also from their own lives and experience. It's a sterile, deadly land.

In the hands of an artist, however, language makes experience more, not less, real. In this case, language makes the book and the experience one. Dennis leaves Los Angeles with "a great, shapeless chunk of experience, the artist's load; bearing it home to his ancient and comfortless shore." Of that experience he will make a work of art very like *The Loved One*, and language, carefully and precisely used, will be his medium.

Helena

After the rousing success of *The Loved One* and the nearly universal celebration of his return to the satiric fold, Waugh knew that his next project, a novel based on the life of Saint Helena, was going to meet some public resistance. He could not, however, resist the urge to write about this woman who, for years, had fascinated him. Through 1949 he persevered with his project and worried about how it would be received. To Nancy Mitford, his favorite confidante, he wrote, "*Helena* . . . is to be my MASTERPIECE. No one will like it at all."[10] The reviewers came close enough to agreeing to hurt his feelings badly.

The *New Statesman* observed, "One cannot help feeling that Waugh has been pulling his punches in this book. A Christian saint and empress is not perhaps the most suitable theme for a satirist who is irrevocably on the side of the angels."[11] *Time* agreed, and added "the religious theme of *Helena* runs close to the ruling passion of Waugh's life, his adopted Roman Catholicism—perhaps too close to it."[12]

Saint Helena, heroine of this short novel, was the mother of the Roman Emperor Constantine the Great. According to legend, she was also the discoverer of the actual cross upon which Christ was crucified. In Waugh's version of the saint's life, Helena is a Briton, the red-haired daughter of an Essex chieftain called Coel. Her classical education has awakened an interest in Rome, and when she falls in love it is with an officer of the Roman legions. She marries him in eager anticipation of traveling with him to "the City," for he is Constantius, protege of the Divine Aurelian and a possible successor to the throne of the Roman Empire. At the time of Helena's marriage, however, the empire has begun its decline, and political intrigue (usually including but not limited to assassinations of emperors by the army) is rife. So the road to Rome is a long one for Helena.

She lives for a brief time at Ratisbon, on the Danube, where she conceives a child, then for about three years at Nish, in what is now southeastern Yugoslavia, where her son Constantine is born. When Constantius is named Governor of Dalmatia, the family relocates to the governor's mansion in that province, on the shores of the Adriatic Sea.

In due course, Constantius is named Caesar (i.e., heir apparent) to Maximian, the emperor of the west. For political reasons, he then divorces Helena and marries Maximian's daughter. Helena lives on in Dalmatia for thirteen years until her son Constantine, now a tribune in Galerius's army, comes to take her away from the impending chaos to the safety of the north. She settles in what is now Trier in West Germany.

Throughout Helena's postings, the practices of the various popular religions of the day, from Mithraism to Gnosticism to Christianity provide much of the social life of her class. While the mysticism of most religions offends her taste for the empirical, she finds in Christian thought a concrete quality and a historical quality that attract her. After the death of Constantius and at about the same time as Constantine puts himself under the protection of Christ and lifts the prohibition on the Christian religion, Helena is baptized.

At the age of seventy, on the occasion of Constantine's jubilee celebration, Helena finally goes to Rome where she meets and associates with a variety of Christians, including the pope. At this time, the issues separating Christians (i.e., whether the father and the son are of the same substance or different substance) seem to her irrelevant, and she decides that what is needed to unify the church is empirical evidence of what seems to her to be the most important fact: "that God became man and died on the Cross."

In pursuit of her proof she travels to Jerusalem, has a dream in which the Wandering Jew shows her the site where the cross was discarded, and recovers the precious relics. Then, as the author notes, "She sailed away, out of authentic history."

Like all of Waugh's novels, *Helena* is very tightly organized. On the simplest level, he uses the life of his heroine as his structural principle, moving from youth to maturity to old age and death. Waugh sees this life of the saint in terms of a journey. From the first moment the reader sees Helena, seated at an upper window listening to her tutor read "the *Iliad* of Homer in a Latin paraphrase," she is in search of "the City." At first her interest is simply in empirical verification of what he has learned. She says, "When I am educated I shall go and find the real Troy—Helen's." In addition, as a citizen of the Roman empire, she is naturally interested in travelling to Rome. In rely to her father's observation that she will hate it, she again demonstrates her empirical bent: "I must see for myself, papa."

Even in her thinking about Rome, however, the young Helena has an unusual notion of what the city represents. She wants it to be inclusive rather than exclusive, as she explains to her condescending husband: "I meant couldn't the wall be at the limits of the world and all men, civilized and barbarian, have a share in the City?" This inclusionary view, dismissed by Constantius as "nonsense," is a clear early signal that for Helena the city is a spiritual rather than a political symbol.

By the time Constantius becomes one of two emperors, Helena sees that the city should be a unifying force in the world, even though her son Constantine points out that Rome is failing as a spiritual center:

Do you know what holds the world together? Not the gods, nor the law nor the army. Simply a name. The fusty old superstitious sanctity of the name of Rome — a bluff two hundred years out of date.

When at the age of seventy or more, Helena reaches Rome, she finds that Constantine's analysis seems to hold. Indeed the

city of Rome is no longer the force that can unify the world.
The city of Rome is the seat of political intrigue and assassina-
tion, much of it the work of Constantine. It is also the home of
the theological debate that threatens the unity of the Christian
church, for example the debate between those who believe that
God the Father and God the Son are identical in substance and
those who believe that God the Father and God the Son are
neither identical nor different in substance, but similar. Rome,
Helena tells Constantine's half-sister Constantia, is "not quite
what I expected."

At this point it becomes clear that the city for which Helena has been seeking is the City of God, that sense of the unity
and oneness of the world that, according to Waugh's vision is
available only to the faithful. And the symbol of that city is
Jerusalem, where Helena travels to find the cross.

Although the spirit of English empiricism motivates Helena's search for the cross, Waugh has no intention of asserting
the historical or natural evidence that Christianity is the one
true religion at the expense of the spiritual or supernatural evidence. Thus what Helena finds in Jerusalem is a vast construction site in such disorder that historical research based on land-
marks and oral history seems doomed to failure. But the
supernatural, in the form of a dream-vision of the Wandering
Jew, leads her at last to her goal — the empirical evidence that
Christ died for mankind, the proof that the City of God is a
reality.

In developing his theme of the search for the heavenly city,
Waugh introduces a number of familiar images, characters, and
ideas: the importance of grace, the superiority of the past over
the present, the importance of language, and nature of the hero.
The treatment of these ideas in *Helena* shows clearly that although the form (a saint's life) is an unusual one for him, this
novel is clearly within the mainstream of Waugh's thought.

Waugh's concern with the problem of grace, that notion
that what one most needs in life (the love of God) cannot be

earned or bargained for, but must be freely given, is illustrated in *Helena* by the contrast between Constantine and Helena. When Constantine explains to his mother that his dark moods are a result of his feeling that he has responsibility for the whole world and that he is separated from everyone in it ("I often feel," he says, "that I am the only real human being in the whole of creation"), she is quick to diagnose his malady: "Power without Grace." That is, she is arguing that by trying to organize the world by an exercise of his own will rather than by subjecting himself fully to the will of God, Constantine separates himself from God and thus from an awareness of how the world is really unified — through faith. Helena understands that to be outside God's grace is spiritually deadening, and thus foresees that the political history of the world, whether it is monarchical or oligarchical or democratic, will be a history of misery, a history of attempts to exercise power without grace.

In contrast to Constantine's state, Helena's triumph is that "she had completely conformed to the will of God." Thus Waugh uses words such as "calm" and "joyful" to describe Helena at her task. Here also Waugh gives his first clear statement of the theme that will be central to his war trilogy: every life has been created for one special purpose, and perfect happiness lies in discovering what that purpose is and fulfilling it. In bringing the cross to the world, Waugh says, Helena had completed "the particular, humble purpose for which she had been created." Helena's sense of herself as acting in accordance with God's will and therefore of being a part of the heavenly city is reflected in her awareness in Rome that she no longer hates the rabble or longs to keep them away. As a part of the heavenly city, "she was in Rome as a pilgrim and she was surrounded by friends."

In *Helena*, as elsewhere in Waugh's work, there is a constant evocation of the decline and fall of the city of man. In contrast to the spiritual history of the world, the secular history represents, in Waugh's view, an appalling record of deterioration.

Historically, the period of Constantine and Helena is perfect grist for Waugh's mill. The Roman Empire lasted less than a century after the death of Constantine, and the coming dissolution can be seen prefigured in the recurrent assassinations and observations such as this one from the Emperor Carus: "They were great men, Claudius and Aurelian. We don't seem to get that type in the army any more." Like Charles Ryder bemoaning the invasion of a world of gentlemen by the Hoopers of the modern age, Carus cannot abide the young men whom he sees about him.

Waugh's distrust of progress, or more accurately, his distrust of what others may consider to be progress, is depicted in Fausta's explanation of what the Council of Nicea was a failure: "I mean, we must have Progress. Homoiousion is definitely dated. *Everyone* who really counts is for Homoousion—or is it the other way round?" To put such a sentiment in the mouth of the foolish Fausta is tantamount to saying directly to the reader that he or she should sympathize instead with those "stupid old diehards" who keep saying, "That's the faith we've been taught."

Finally, Waugh's sense that the world is in decline is caught beautifully in the scene in which the Wandering Jew offers to show Helena where the cross is hidden at no charge. He reasons that popularizing Christianity will be good for his business, selling religious artifacts:

Helena listened and in her mind's eye, clear as all else on that brilliant timeless morning, what was in store. She saw the sanctuaries of Christendom become a fair ground, stalls hung with beads and medals, substances yet unknown pressed into sacred emblems; heard a chatter of haggling in tongues yet unspoken. She saw the treasuries of the Church filled with forgeries and impostures. She saw Christians fighting and stealing to get possession of trash.

Waugh's distrust of progress and his concern about the tendency of the world to deteriorate is ameliorated in *Helena* to some extent by the contrast between the spiritual strand and the earthly strand in the novel. In the character of Helena, in her triumph in finding the cross, and in the last image which likens her to a hunter who puts the hounds back on the scent, Waugh is able to find a hopeful conclusion for his novel, even though the earthly context, the context of the Roman Empire, suggests imminent doom.

One of the difficulties for a serious reader of *Helena* is the presentation of Helena herself. As the protagonist, she is central and her character is consistently in the foreground. She is also an utterly unconvincing fourth century character. Instead, Waugh makes her into a charming British matron of his own age. In doing so, he gives her the virtues of the British heroes he consistently finds admirable: a classical education, a taste for riding, a strong streak of common sense, and a feeling of responsibility for her land and her retainers.

Waugh deals with the importance of language (in the form of style) at two points in *Helena*, and in doing so gives the reader particular insight into his motivation in writing this book. Of course, it was a work of love, but, as the reviewers noted, it did seem a curious undertaking for Waugh. In the character of Lactantius, however, one sees Waugh's self portrait. Like Waugh, Lactantius is a great stylist:

He delighted in writing, in the joinery and embellishment of his sentences, in the consciousness of high rare virtue when every word had been used in its purest and most precise sense, in the kitten games of syntax and rhetoric.

As a stylist, Lactantius appreciates the power of the pen and anticipates, with some misgivings, the coming of Edward Gibbon, author of *The Decline and Fall of the Roman Empire*, whose attitude toward Christianity is most charitably described as skeptical. Lactantius foresees the coming of

an apostate of my own trade, a false historian, with the mind of Cicero or Tacitus and the soul of an animal. . . . A man like that might make it his business to write down the martyrs and excuse the persecutors. He might be refuted again and again but what he wrote would remain in people's minds when the refutations were quite forgotten. That is what style does—it has the Egyptian secret of the embalmers.

And in *Helena*, Waugh is attempting to use his style to set the record straight and to create a refutation that will be as powerful as Gibbon's assertions.

One can be quite sure that Lactantius's false historian is meant to be Gibbon for two reasons. At the beginning of the chapter in which the discussion of style takes place, Helena has been presented with "an Indian ape, the expensive present of a visiting diplomat." At the point where the false historian is described as having "the soul of an animal," the ape rattles his chain and is identified by the narrator as a gibbon. In addition, at the close of the novel, Waugh describes the church where Helena is buried as the very place where "Edward Gibbon later sat and *premeditated* his history" (italics mine). Clearly Gibbon is the adversary here, and in this contest between two versions of history, style is the weapon.

5

The War Trilogy

Men at Arms

When *Men at Arms* appeared in 1952, advertised as the first volume of a trilogy, the critical reception was mixed. Critics had already begun the practice of reviewing Waugh instead of his books, and the notices of *Men at Arms* contain a variety of negative references to Waugh's religious enthusiasm and his "snobbishness." Cyril Connolly, writing for the *Sunday Times of London*, noted that "for the first time I found myself bored by the central section of a Waugh novel." He continued, "Where I feel Mr. Waugh has gone wrong . . . is in failing to build up the relationships between his military characters, who do not exist in the round."[1] The *New Statesman* began by declaring, "As a novel, *Men at Arms* is not nearly as good as *Put Out More Flags*. As a 'novel of military life,' it is uproariously and unflaggingly funny." The reviewer went on to criticize what he took to be Waugh's tendency to ". . . depict Mother Church as one Big Dorm and her mysteries as so much sacred larking."[2] The most consistently positive review was in *Time* magazine, where the writer saw Waugh broadening and deepening his efforts to express two sides of his nature: "Reading *Men at Arms*," he wrote, "is like hearing a full keyboard used by a pianist who has hitherto confined himself to a single octave."[3] The most forthrightly negative response may have been that of the *New Republic*. Having announced that Waugh had committed the satirist's suicide—falling in love with his subject—and having accused him of becoming maudlin, Joseph Frank concluded: "I should like, therefore, to propose a judicious division of labor. Let God look after the well-being of the Anglo-Catholic aristocracy, and let Evelyn Waugh, to the continuing delight of his readers, return to their follies and their foibles."[4]

Waugh's own assessment of *Men at Arms* varied a bit while the work was in progress, and remained apologetic after it was completed. He mentioned it often in letters to friends while he was at work on it. To Nancy Mitford he wrote, "My novel is unreadable & endless. Nothing but tippling in officer's messes and drilling on barrack squares. No demon sex. No blood or thunder."[5] Five months later he wrote to Clarissa Churchill, "I have finished a novel—slogging, inelegant, the first volume of four or five, which won't show any shape until the end."[6] When he wrote to Lady Mary Lygon in the same month, however, he seemed to be enjoying the entire project more: "I have written a book in poor taste, mostly about WCs and very very dull. Well, it is a dull subject, isn't it. The only exciting moment is when a WC blows up with Capt. Apthorpe sitting on it. The shock & shame drive him mad. He is the hero."[7]

When the book was complete, Waugh's sense of failure seems to have solidified. He wrote to Graham Greene, "I finished that book I was writing. *Not* good. Of course all writers write some bad books but it seems a pity at this particular time. It has some excellent farce, but only for a few pages. The rest very dull. Well, the war was like that."[8] To Nancy Mitford, he wrote "I have re-read my forth-coming book—awfully bad."[9] It seems safe to say, at this distant remove, that much of his worry was misplaced, for *Men at Arms* is not a dull book. It is, however, different from anything Waugh had attempted before.

Men at Arms is the first volume of Waugh's war trilogy, a set which also includes *Officers and Gentlemen* and *Unconditional Surrender* (called *The End of the Battle* in the United States). Set in 1939, the novel focuses on one unhappy English Catholic and his responses to the outbreak of World War II. Guy Crouchback has lived for eight years at Castello Crouchback, a family residence in Italy. He is divorced and sees no way to remarry because of the teachings of his church. He thus seems destined to be the end of his family line. The outbreak of the war stirs him from his lethargy and offers him an opportunity to serve his country and, he thinks, the cause of justice. He leaves Italy for England immediately.

In book one, "Apthorpe Gloriosus" (Apthorpe Vainglorious), Guy makes several attempts to join the military but is unsuccessful until he meets Major Tickeridge of the Halberdiers, who arranges for him to join a group of officers in training. The first days of Halberdier training are idyllic for Guy. He learns to love the traditions and decorum of the corps, he idolizes his superiors, and he feels accepted by his peers. Among the probationary officers, his best friend is Apthorpe, a "burly, tanned, moustached" man of about his own age, who, until recently, has been in Africa. Apthorpe's fetish is "equipment."

The first disruption of Guy's idyll is the injury to his knee that occurs when the officers play an impromptu game of rugby in the dining room. The second and more serious disruption comes when the probationary officers are sent away from the barracks to Kut-al-Imara House, a boy's school that has been taken over as a training center. Here everything is different. The regular officers are inconsiderate and definitely not awe inspiring. The instruction is aimless and poorly delivered. The accommodations are uninviting, and the dining room is always deserted. Guy begins to fall out of love with the corps, but he is saved by the arrival of Colonel Ben Ritchie-Hook, who takes over the training. At about the same time Guy hears a theological argument that allows him to believe that his ex-wife Virginia is still morally his wife and that it is appropriate for him to go to bed with her. He advances this argument when they meet and is rejected again.

In book two, "Apthorpe Furibundus" (Apthorpe Furious), Colonel Ritchie-Hook takes over the training of the probationary officers; it consists mostly of instruction in the art of "biffing" the enemy. Apthorpe and Ritchie-Hook are involved in a long battle of wills over the possession of one of Apthorpe's more elaborate pieces of equipment, a portable chemical toilet he calls his "Thunder-box." The joke culminates in Ritchie-Hook's booby-trapping the contraption and exploding it with Apthorpe on it.

At the end of the training, Apthorpe is made a company commander and Guy, who has anticipated greater success, is made a platoon commander, two levels below company commander. He is demoralized until he learns that he is being prepared to lead men in battle while Apthorpe is being trained as an administrator. When the Halberdiers are finally ordered to sail for France, it looks as if the new officers will all be left behind. At the last minute, however, they are rescued by Ben Ritchie-Hook, and Guy is made a company commander at last.

Book three, "Apthorpe Immolatus" (Apthorpe Sacrificed), opens with the Halberdiers on two hour notice to sail to combat. Guy is learning his trade. His nephew Tony is taken prisoner at Calais. The brigade finally sails for Dakar to help mop up. Disappointed at the peripheral role assigned them, Ritchie-Hook organizes a landing party to be commanded by Guy. Ritchie-Hook goes along in disguise, however, kills and beheads an African, gets wounded, and lands Guy and himself in trouble. Just as it looks as if Guy might escape disciplinary action, Apthorpe falls ill and is taken to the hospital. Guy visits him and takes a bottle of whisky as a gift. When Apthorpe drinks it all at once and dies as a result, Guy is in trouble again. The novel ends with Guy and Ritchie-Hook leaving the battalion to return to England.

Officers and Gentlemen

The reception of *Officers and Gentlemen* was also mixed, with many reviewers openly lamenting Waugh's attempt to develop a new style. Those who liked the work claimed to understand that he was undertaking a new task, while those who disliked it repeatedly advised him to return to the satirical farces that had made his name. Christopher Sykes, reviewing the book positively for *Time and Tide*, wrote, "A primary rule of style is broken: farce is mixed with comedy, with tragi-comedy, and even with tragedy. Well, the only question worth asking is whether this matters. It does not matter a bit. The result is abundantly successful."[10] Cyril Connolly, another old friend, begged to differ: "Mr. Waugh," he observed, "used to be a satirist, the possessor of a ferocious private weapon which he did not hesitate to use. . . . in this novel a new element of amiability, even of what might be called Christian charity, informs the pages. This I find absolutely delightful, but not conducive to satire."[11] Kingsley Amis differed even more strongly, fearing in print that Waugh was finished as a satirist: ". . .Mr. Waugh is unwilling—I cannot believe that he is unable—to chance his arm and have a go and lay us in the aisles. . . . The next novel in the series will show whether Mr. Waugh's invention is really impaired. . . . I cannot believe that it is."[12]

Waugh's response to the less than enthusiastic reviews was not good humored. He wrote to Sir Maurice Bowra, "I am awfully encouraged that you like *Officers & Gentlemen*. The reviewers don't, fuck them,"[13] and in a letter to Christopher Sykes he explained what was wrong with young literary types such as Kingsley Amis: ". . . they all read English Literature for schools and so take against it, while good critics & writers read as a treat and a relaxation from Latin & Greek."[14] In his diary he noted, "I am quite complacent about the book's quality. My only anxiety is about American sales."[15] Educating a large family and preparing to "bring out" his eldest daughter was putting a severe strain on Waugh's finances, and he thought it would be "very convenient to have another success."[16]

Officers and Gentlemen chronicles Guy's efforts to fulfill his promise to deliver Apthorpe's equipment to Chatty Corner, a friend from Apthorpe's African days; Guy's adventures in Scotland training with Tommy Blackhouse's X Commando; and the participation of Hookforce in the invasion and evacuation of Crete. Like *Men at Arms*, it concludes with Guy's return to the Halberdier Barracks, exiled from his brigade once more.

The first section of the novel, "Happy Warriors," opens with a comic description of the bombing of London and the response of the denizens of Bellamy's to the air raids. Separated from his battalion by his two mistakes in Africa (the unauthorized raiding party with Ben Ritchie-Hook and the gift of a bottle of whisky that killed Apthorpe), Guy finds himself back in England where no one, including the Halberdiers, is expecting him. He is given leave to try to find Apthorpe's heir, Chatty Corner. Almost as soon as he is beyond reach, the army begins to look for him, and the wonderfully characterized Colonel "Jumbo" Trotter is dispatched to search him out and deliver him to H.O.O.HQ— Hazardous Offensive Operations Headquarters. At H.O.O.HQ, Guy, with his "service car, a three-ton lorry, an RASC driver, a Halberdier servant and a full Colonel," is ordered to the Isle of Mugg to join the X Commando, a group Waugh defines as "a military unit, about the size of a battalion, composed of volunteers for special service." In X Commando, the volunteers are mostly friends of the commander, Tommy Blackhouse, who is Virginia's second husband and the man for whom she left Guy.

At X Commando, Guy finds Chatty Corner, now known as King Kong because he has been hired to teach mountaineering and rock climbing to the unit. He also rediscovers Trimmer, now called McTavish, one of the original group of probationary officers who was dismissed from the Halberdiers when Ritchie-Hook took over the training. And he meets Ivor Claire, the affected, young, beautiful, talented horseman and natural leader who strikes Guy as "the fine flower of them all. . . quintessential England, the man Hitler had not taken into account."

While X Commando trains, Guy struggles through a formal dinner with Hector Campbell, the Laird of Mugg, a deaf and slightly mad old Scot who keeps looking for explosives to clear a bathing beach so he can make the cold and inhospitable island into a resort. He manages to escape being made part of a mad nutritionist's attempt to demonstrate that men can survive off the land; and, when Ritchie-Hook appears to declare that X Commando is now part of Hookforce, Guy is named brigade intelligence officer and happily sails for Crete.

In the meantime, Guy's father is teaching classics to Catholic boys, worrying his way through the morality of negotiated approaches to sending gifts to prisoners of war (of which Tony Box-Bender is one), and confounding with his goodness the owners of the hotel who wish to take away his sitting room so they can rent it to someone else for a higher price.

Trimmer and Virginia meet in Glasgow where he, on leave from X Commando, is impersonating a major and she, tired and unhappy and recently deserted by a boyfriend who "went off quite suddenly," is alone and short of money. They become intimate, and Trimmer conceives an unrequited passion for her.

A brief section entitled "Interlude" makes the transition from the Isle of Mugg to the Middle East, introduces Ivor Claire's Corporal-Major Ludovic, and establishes that Ritchie-Hook and his landing force have disappeared into the interior.

Book two, "In the Picture," finds Guy and Hookforce under the command of Major Hound who "had chosen a military career because he was not clever enough to pass into the civil service." While Hookforce is stationed in Egypt, Julia Stitch appears. Through her, Guy learns Hookforce is bound for Crete. Looking forward to the adventure of "raiding lines of communication on the Greek mainland," Hookforce instead finds itself charged with covering the withdrawal of all other allied troops on the island. The plan is for the navy to evacuate all forces except Hookforce and for Hookforce to be taken prisoner or to escape on its own in small boats. In the process of covering the evacuation, Ivor Claire deserts; Major Hound disappears, presumably killed by Ludovic; and Ludovic and Guy escape with a small group in an open boat. In order to protect Ivor, whom she thinks Guy intends to denounce for his desertion, Mrs. Stitch arranges to have Guy sent back to England on a slow boat. At about the same time, Russia joins the Western alliance, and Guy sees once again that justice and order have nothing to do with this world "where priests were spies and gallant friends proved traitors and his country was led blundering into dishonour."

While Hookforce is being decimated in the Middle East, Trimmer is becoming a hero. In a public relations assault intended to create a lower-class hero, Trimmer, accompanied by Ian Kilbannock, an air force publicist, leads his group of sappers in an assault on the uninhabited Isle of Jersey. They get lost in the fog and land on the mainland of France; Trimmer shoots at a barking dog and then runs back to the beach, intending to leave his men stranded. Ian, however, keeps him there until the men reappear, having blown up a railroad bed. Trimmer becomes a national hero and is about to be sent around the country on a speaking tour. He is also driving Virginia mad with his unwelcome passion for her.

Unconditional Surrender

Although Waugh once claimed that *Officers and Gentlemen* completed the story begun in *Men at Arms*, he later confessed that he had always known a third volume was needed. When that third volume, *Unconditional Surrender* (called *The End of the Battle* in the United States), appeared in 1961, its reception was as varied as the receptions of the first two. What was unusual was the strength of feeling with which the critics received this work. Kingsley Amis sounded the battle cry of snobbery again, pointing out what he considered to be inconsistencies in the application of values to the behavior of various characters and summarizing, "The Crouchback motto is . . . *'It's all right when I do it'*."[17] Philip Toynbee deplored the same tendency in the novel: "In Mr. Waugh's present book almost everyone is odious except for a few members of old and dignified Catholic families." In addition, he berated Waugh for using positive instruction: "unlike the true satirist, Mr. Waugh has again been rash enough to give us a loving picture of what, by contrast, *ought* to be admired."[18]

On the other hand, Cyril Connolly not only praised *Unconditional Surrender* but through it was led to reconsider his earlier negative responses to *Men at Arms* and *Officers and Gentlemen*. He found that "the cumulative effect is most impressive, and it seems to me unquestionably the finest novel to come out of the war."[19] Bernard Bergonzi, writing for the *Guardian*, also found only good things to say: "*Unconditional Surrender* seems to me Mr. Waugh's best book since *The Loved One*. It is exciting, too, because it makes much more sense of the first two volumes of the military trilogy; the whole work now looks a substantial achievement, and one which may alter our total picture of Mr. Waugh's writing."[20] What Connolly, Bergonzi, and V. S. Pritchett saw in *Unconditional Surrender* and in the trilogy as a whole was that Waugh had undertaken and executed a serious and complex project, that for the first time he had combined social satire, political satire, and religious apologetics in the body of a fictional work, and that he done it successfully.

If Waugh had been right in 1955 and if *Unconditional Surrender* had never been written, readers would leave Guy Crouchback much as they found him—lonely, isolated, despairing of the modern world. But the final novel of the trilogy fulfills the implications of the first two volumes and brings the comic structure to completion.

The novel has a five-part structure, comprising a prologue, three books, and an epilogue. The prologue, "Locust Years," places Guy back in England, left behind once more by the Halberdiers who have embarked for the battle. In hopes of finding a contribution he can make, he joins Jumbo Trotter, now "Commandant of Number 6 Transit Camp," in London and succeeds in becoming Tommy Blackhouse's liaison officer at H.O.O.HQ. But the real importance of the prologue is Mr. Crouchback's letter to his son. In it the saintly father sounds the theme of the novel: In considerations of a theological nature, "Quantitative judgments don't apply."

Book one, "State Sword," like *Officers and Gentlemen*, opens with a crowded London street, but this time the crowd is standing in line to see the Sword of Stalingrad, a gift from the people of England to the people of Stalingrad. Ludovic, now an officer, stops to see it on his way to call on his benefactor, Sir Ralph Brompton, and then his publisher, Everard Spruce; Ludovic's *Pensees* are about to be published. At Spruce's, Ludovic meets Guy, whom he thinks knows of Ludovic's murders of Major Hound and the delirious sapper during the escape from Crete.

Guy is working in H.O.O.HQ where a civilian efficiency expert has installed an electronic personnel selector. This magical machine, when asked for "an officer for special employment; under forty, with a university degree, who has lived in Italy and had Commando training," identifies Guy as the only nominee. Guy is thrilled by the opportunity to return to battle.

In the meantime, Virginia is in trouble. Her American husband has divorced her; she has spent two miserable years with Trimmer, keeping his spirits up; and she is now alone and pregnant.

Book two is called "Fin de Ligne" (The End of the Line). As it opens, Mr. Crouchback dies at Matchet. At his funeral Guy finally comes to understand his duty to God and the necessity devoting himself to those services that only he can perform.

As a part of his training for "special employment," Guy is posted to a parachute training camp administered by now Major Ludovic who takes heroic measures to avoid him. In the same class is Frank de Souza, one of the original class of Halberdier probationary officers and now a communist. Although he is game and brave in parachute training, Guy injures his knee in his first jump and is invalided back to London where his uncle Peregrine invites him to convalesce at his apartment. Hoping that Guy will be killed, Ludovic recommends him for combat duty even though he has not completed the training course.

In the meantime, Virginia has discovered that she is pregnant with Trimmer's child. After several attempts to find an abortionist, she gives up and decides to find a husband instead. Recalling Guy's attempted seduction of her at Claridge's during his first days with the Halberdiers, she seeks him out. Guy recognizes that he no longer loves Virginia, but he also recognizes that marrying her and thus providing a father for her child is an act of charity that only he can perform. So he does.

Book three, "The Death Wish," chronicles the last campaign of Guy Crouchback. In it he is posted to Yugoslavia to provide support for the partisans in their opposition to the Germans. At his post, he discovers a community of 108 exiled Jews who want to get to Italy where they can contact Jewish relief agencies. When the United Nations Relief and Rehabilitation Administration (UNRRA) indicates an interest in displaced persons, Guy seizes the opportunity to take up the cause of the Jews. However, his efforts are thwarted. When, after a long wait, the airplanes come to pick up the refugees, it's too foggy for them to land. The supplies that are sent in to see them through the winter when they can't be evacuated incite jealousy in the peasants and the partisans and actually exacerbate the Jews' problems. Guy's constant attempts to help the Jews finally result in his recall from Yugoslavia, and his parting gift of American magazines to Madame Kanyi results in her execution as a traitor.

The Jews are not Guy's only concern in Yugoslavia. De Souza appears mysteriously to prepare the way for a visit to the partisans by an American and a British general who are to assess the effectiveness of the partisan troops. The British officer is Major-General Ritchie-Hook, now aged and enfeebled, and looking for one last hurrah. When the partisans pull back from their planned attack on a blockhouse because of the approach of two German scout cars, Ritchie-Hook attacks the blockhouse alone and is killed at the foot of the wall.

Meanwhile in England, Virginia converts to Catholicism, gives birth to a son whom she names Gervase, and is killed, with Uncle Peregrine, when a bomb strikes his apartment block. Her child is placed in the care of Guy's sister, Angela, and later in the care of the child's godmother, Eloise Plessington.

Ludovic, too, has a death wish, but his is a novel. After the publication of his *Pensees*, Ludovic writes a long "very gorgeous, almost gaudy, tale of romance and high drama." The title is *The Death Wish* and the consensus is that it is nonsense. But it is wonderfully successful.

The epilogue, "The Festival of Britain," takes place in 1951, seven years after Guy's return from Yugoslavia. Guy has married Domenica Plessington, the kind of Catholic girl he should have married in the first place, and they and the child Gervase live at Broome in the agent's house. Ludovic has bought the Castello with the profits from *The Death Wish*; Guy's pompous brother-in-law, Arthur Box-Bender, has lost his seat in Parliament; and Tony Box-Bender, Guy's nephew, has entered a monastery.

Guy Crouchback was a boisterous and lively child who chased leaves with his mother in the fall, playing that each one he caught would ensure such and such a time of happiness. Now, however, he lives alone, and has little sympathy with mankind. He considers himself to be spiritually dry and emotionally wounded. He doesn't socialize easily, but he enjoys it when people draw him out (as guest nights). His affections for the officers of the Halberdiers and X Commando succeed for a while in drawing him into human activity, and that when they "betray" his idealism, he again retreats.

The reclusive strain runs in the family. In Ivo it was exaggerated enough to be fatal. In Guy, the tendency is there, as it is in Tony Box-Bender, but it does not develop pathologically. Why? The answer is grace, I think, and Waugh's notion that at certain times one is particularly open to the operations of grace. For Guy these times come in *Unconditional Surrender*, when he is finally healed. In the wonderfully ambiguous revelation that Guy is finally becoming spiritually whole, Waugh writes:

Without passion or sentiment but in a friendly, cosy way, they had resumed the pleasures of marriage and in the weeks while his knee mended the deep old wound in Guy's heart and pride mended also, as perhaps Virginia had intuitively known that it might do.

This is indeed an odd sentence. In the first two clauses we have what appears to be two statements of fact: Virginia came back to his bed and his wounds were healed. In the final clause, ". . .as perhaps Virginia had intuitively known that it might do . . .," we have three forceful words which do not all point the sentence in the same direction: *perhaps*, *might*, and *known*.

Of all Waugh's heroes, Guy Crouchback is arguably the greatest exile. At the opening of *Men at Arms*, Guy is in residence at Castello Crouchback in Italy, cut off from his family, his exwife, his country, and, in many ways, his faith. In fact, he is cut off from mankind, for he is not simpatico. Guy, Waugh tells the reader, is "set apart from his fellows by his own deep wound," which is like the wound of the fisher-king in T. S. Eliot's "The Waste Land," in that it results in physical and spiritual sterility. For Guy, neither love of man nor love of God has been strong enough to overcome the debilitating effects of his wound.

And what is the nature of Guy's wound? Eight years earlier, when Guy was twenty-seven years old, his wife left him for another man. She was, the narrator tells us, "a bright, fashionable girl" but "not a Catholic," and Guy was the youngest son in the last of a Catholic line that had occupied its countryseat "in uninterrupted male succession since the reign of Henry I." In Guy's family there had been three sons and one daughter, but the eldest son was killed in World War I and the second starved himself to death in 1931; Guy alone remained to carry on the name. When his wife left him, Guy was marooned: he could not remarry and he had no wife to bear him sons. This inability to perpetuate the family name is part of the sterility of his life.

For all his devotion to his religion, Guy finds no solace and no sense of communion in it. He may take communion, but he does not feel it. The narrator observes, "Even in his religion he felt no brotherhood." It is as if Virginia's leaving him had resulted in a spiritual death as well as an emotional death. Guy holds to the forms of Catholicism, for example in refusing to remarry and in going to confession before undertaking a journey, but the forms do not nurture him.

Guy's spiritual exile is perhaps best symbolized by his alienation from his fellows. Even in the simplest situations, Guy is too disengaged from the life around him to bother communicating with others. Leaving Italy, he is conscious that he is not simpatico, that his neighbors and acquaintances weep at his departure less because they love him than because weeping is what form requires. He spends his time on the way to the train trying to decide how to dispose of the cake his servants have made for him; he cannot be bothered to discuss politics with the fascist taxidriver ("Guy had no wish to persuade or convince or to share his opinions with anyone" MA,); and he cannot even bring himself to say "Here's how" when Major Tickeridge proposes a toast.

It is the contrast of Guy's situation with that of Gervase and Hermione in the opening pages of the work that defines the source of his problem: he is without love—of family, of home, of God, and thus of life. It is Guy's joining the Halberdiers that sets him on his way to recovery.

Although Guy's spiritual malaise provides the most dramatic case of exile, it is not the only one. His plight is mirrored in the situations of Sir Roger of Waybroke and his own father, Gervase Crouchback. Mr. Crouchback, exiled from his home but not from his family or his faith, is illustrative of an alternative way for Guy to cope with his own exile. Where Guy has become withdrawn and unable to participate in human endeavor, Mr. Crouchback carries on and, in fact, assumes the role of teacher to another generation of young Catholics.

Sir Roger of Waybroke, an English knight killed at Santa Dulcina en route to Jerusalem in the second crusade, is also an exile, and it is appropriate that he should become Guy's patron. The story of Sir Roger suggests early in the trilogy that Guy's religion can still offer him some hope of a happy ending, even if it is not to be the one for which he had hoped. The crusaders believed that if they died in the holy land, fighting for the faith, they would go directly to heaven. Although Sir Roger failed to reach Jerusalem, he has become "the English saint," a fate he could not have foreseen.

In addition to the spiritual malaise brought on by the lack of love in Guy's life at the novel's opening, there is the sense of exile resulting from his alienation from the modern age. The public side of his private alienation is found in his longing to have the modern world acknowledge that such a thing as justice exists, that right and wrong exist. Thus the war, which tends to simplify, at least initially, seems to offer salvation, to make sense of the moral system, and to offer a chance to become a part of some worthwhile action. The German-Russian nonaggression pact, which seems to put the godless communists on the side of the Nazis, lets him think of the war as a crusade. However, when the Russians join the West, his system for valuing what is happening in the world is temporarily disabled. He cannot understand how the West can ally itself with those who persecute the religious. Thus the partisans in *Unconditional Surrender* are the recipients of the loathing both Guy and Waugh feel for the enemies of Christianity. The sense of injury Guy feels is exacerbated by his belief that the British have become part of an unholy alliance.

Sadly for Guy, it seems not to be possible in a Waugh novel to cure a spiritual ailment with a secular treatment. In order to achieve the sense of oneness with the world for which he longs, Guy must learn, among other things, to value himself as a spiritual being. His early despair and sense of his own lack of worth is clear in his constant references to himself as "fodder," "ready now for immediate consumption," "an extra mouth," and "destitute, possessed of nothing save a few dry grains of faith." He thinks he would like to sacrifice himself to some greater good, and it seems logical to him that he should be sacrificed because he is flawed. Greater goods, however, always insist on the best for sacrifices, not the worst. For Guy to make the worthy sacrifice he needs to heal his wound (and, he hopes, to help heal the world's wounds), he must first become aware that he is worth something, in some way, himself. This is the truth he discovers when he attends church with Angela and Tony and hears the words of the canon: "Domine non sum dignus" (Lord, I am not worthy).

Waugh uses "Domine non sum dignus" to explain Guy's sense of his own worthlessness in the world. This is interesting because while the phrase clearly means precisely that, it comes from the communion service in which Christ's "full, perfect, and sufficient" sacrifice is celebrated as having been made, through God's manifold and great mercies, for the benefit of mankind that is, by nature, unworthy of it. It is God's mercy alone that makes man worthy; nothing that man can do without God matters. This is the importance of the notion of grace in Guy's religion and in the trilogy—that mankind does not have to be worthy. Divine love and protection are given freely, not earned. When Guy can learn to ask for them instead of saying "I don't ask anything from you," he may have them, for as Mr. Crouchback explains, the church does not stand on its dignity, but welcomes one "at the first sign of compunction." In addition, it is part of the mystical nature of divine love that feeling it gives Guy the possibility of taking action in the world.

The war trilogy, then, is the story of Guy's spiritual progress from exile to participating member of the faith. His journey is not without detours, and his progress takes place on many levels at one time. For example, he moves from immaturity to maturity, from a romantic view of the world to a realistic view, from alienation to integration, as well as from "spiritual dryness" to grace. On every level, however, his progress is an amelioration of his exile, so that the essence of the war trilogy is a celebration of coming home—to family, to England, and to God.

In *Men at Arms*, as Jeffrey Heath points out, Apthorpe serves as foil to the overwrought, immature, and romantic Guy.[21] The two men are the same age when they join the Halberdiers, they are both immediately dubbed "Uncle," and they both injure their knees during training. They are also both caught up in a thoroughly imaginary world. What they expect of the military is too much for any real unit to provide—romance, adventure, heroic opportunities. But these are the stuff of boy's stories, not of everyday life in a modern military machine.

That Guy and Apthorpe are both immature is established by Waugh's choice of training site; he sends them to a boy's school where Guy can relive his adolescence. Without the joyous Ritchie-Hook to ensure that the anarchic spirit lives, adolescence at a public school proves to be no more enjoyable the second time around than the first. The food is terrible, the masters (in this case the training officers) are incompetent or at least boring, and the desire to escape defeats any hope of building a team spirit. Even when Ritchie-Hook arrives, the probationary officers feel like schoolboys when the headmaster is "in a wax."

As the novel progresses, Guy becomes a little more mature, although he remains in thrall to his boy's book notion of heroism. The rebuff by Virginia, when he tries to seduce her in the name of the primacy of the church, sobers him a little, but the visit of the Loamshire officers and his conviction that they are German infiltrators who are going to kill him and capture his camp shows that his imagination is running wild. He is becoming more responsible, however, and is beginning to see through his own imaginary constructs. Apthorpe, on the other hand, becomes steadily more committed to the vision of the corps he brought with him. Apthorpe's movement away from maturity can be seen in his preoccupation with his "equipment," his desire to draw Guy into a secret association from which all others are excluded (when he makes Guy cokeeper of the "thunder box"), and his insistence on being saluted after his promotion. But as Guy comes to take the juvenile aspects of their situation less seriously, Apthorpe takes them more seriously. When he interferes with the training of the signal corps and uses Morse code to issue a challenge to their officer, the reader cannot help but feel that Apthorpe is becoming more childish and outrageous by the minute. Even his death, which follows Guy's final disenchantment with the Captain Truslove mentality, results from a childish lack of restraint—it is not the whisky that kills him, but his drinking all of the whisky at once.

Throughout *Men at Arms* the reader feels that Apthorpe is playing a part. He is almost too well cast to be taken seriously, being "burly, tanned, moustached, primed with a rich vocabulary of military terms and abbreviations." Although his greatest concern just before he dies is to keep his gear out of the hands of the "high-church boy-scouts" to whom his aunt would almost assuredly give it, he is not much more than a high-church boy-scout himself, with his delight in confidential texts, special ointments, and waterproof matchboxes. We are delighted by the information, but not truly surprised when Chatty Corner reveals in *Officers and Gentlemen* that Apthorpe was never a big game hunter after all, but a city-bound tobacco clerk.

Apthorpe's death does not actually signal the end of Guy's immaturity, but it does suggest that a stage has been passed and that Guy should be less subject to the delusions based on a view of the world as romance than he was in the past. When he is instructed to return to England, one feels less that he has reached home than that he is returning to the starting line to try the route once more. He is still an exile.

In *Officers and Gentlemen*, Guy gives up his illusion that the world can be made meaningful by the actions of the heroes of myth and legend, or even their modern counterparts, the Captain Trusloves of the imaginary world. He continues, however, to cling to the notion that the war represents a conflict between the civilized, Christian moral world and the world of pure evil as epitomized by the Nazis and the godless communists. In the person of Ivor Claire, Guy finds a new double and a new reason for hope. Ivor, he tells himself, embodies all that is decent and brave in the British aristocracy. Through Ivor and men like him, the cause of England, which is the cause of justice, will prevail.

Ivor Claire is a captain of the Blues, the familiar name of the very prestigious Regiment of Royal Horse Guards. He has been seconded to X Commando and, thus, comes to command a troop of Hookforce men. He is handsome, educated, a good rider, and a friend of people who are high in government, for example, Ambassador and Mrs. Stitch. He is not averse to making money by playing high-stakes poker, nor to commandeering a bus to carry his training troop to a rendezvous. He is too clever to be reprimanded and also too clever to be trustworthy. But he is very cool, even under the eye of his commander, Tommy Blackhouse, and his troops love him for it. His position is rather like that of a sophisticated upperclassman who leads his inferiors into schemes they could never have developed for themselves.

As Guy supposes, Ivor's troops would follow him anywhere. Unfortunately, Ivor's destiny is to go where his troops cannot follow, because he abandons them. In the midst of the battle in Crete, Ivor appears at Guy's cave to discuss the order to stay and be taken prisoner. Like Guy, Ivor is distanced from his fellows; however, he lacks the dedication to his men that Halberdier training has fostered in Guy. He also demonstrates a concern for self that almost succeeds in hiding the fact that he has a troop of men for whom he is responsible. In a position that seems to call for a far greater sense of responsibility than Guy has had thrust upon him, Ivor fails. When he walks up the long hill to honor, as he says to Guy, he finds himself near a ship that will lead him away from danger and away from the interminable hours he would find in a prisoner-of-war camp.

Ivor's story, like the story of the British acceptance of the Russians as allies seems to Guy to be a story of betrayal. The decision of this romantic captain of one of England's most romantic regiments to desert his men and find his own way home is no less devastating than the decision of Britain to accept the Russian persecutors of eastern European Catholics into the Western alliance.

With the acceptance of the Russians and the defection of Ivor, Guy comes to understand that the way to fellowship is not through commitment to some public sense of duty, but through private or personal commitment. In the retreat from Crete he has seen, if he had not before, that institutions (here the military) are incapable of preserving either personal or public honor. In his reflections about the circumstances under which Tommy Blackhouse might have pursued Ivor Claire, Guy begins to understand the necessary difference between public and private issues. If Tommy had caught Ivor endangering the lives of other men, he might have shot him on the spot. But as Ivor has escaped, and as his situation now has no influence on the lives of the men with whose welfare he was charged, Tommy is simply not interested. For Tommy, it is a question of efficiency. For Guy, however, efficiency is not the issue. He is fighting a war for justice, and he is devastated by the cowardly behavior of his friend. He is also wounded by what might be construed as his own cowardly behavior, for although he offers his group the chance to attempt escape in the open boat and although his responsibility for them is less than Ivor's for his group, the narrator opines that Guy left behind "an immeasurable piece of his manhood" when he left Crete. In the response of his government to the invasion of Russia by the Germans and in Tommy Blackhouse's response to the desertion of Ivor Claire, Guy finds more than enough reason to reject the notion that public honor is something with which a man can legitimately be concerned.

At this point in the trilogy, it begins to look as if Guy's

experience will be wholly negative. Whatever he attempts and from whatever motive, he manages to "blot his copybook." The raid on Dakar was well managed except for the injury to Ritchie-Hook; the visit to Apthorpe was well meant and would never have resulted in such disaster without the help of the brigade major who later disclaimed all responsibility. In the episode on Crete, Guy is the only Hookforce officer who seems to remain both competent and alive. Major Hound quickly becomes unable to work in such a confusing environment, and Guy is forced to carry orders to and from a man who understands not at all what is happening. Whether Guy's departure from Crete in the open boat is reprehensible or not (and one guesses not, because Tommy Blackhouse seems to think he should be put in for a military cross), he seems to have behaved bravely and in a way that does not disgrace his Halberdier training. But to save Ivor Claire's reputation, Guy must be sent home in what seems to be disgrace. Once again, he is an exile.

Unconditional Surrender opens with Guy having spent two years "soldiering on" with the Halberdiers. Having been left behind as too old when his brigade sailed for battle, Guy searches for a way to participate in the struggle. When he is assigned to a project that will ultimately lead to his serving as a liaison with the Yugoslavian partisans, he enters Ludovic's sphere, and Ludovic becomes his double in the final novel.

Ludovic's movement in *Unconditional Surrender* is from classicist to romantic, from control to lack of control. When his *Pensees* are published, they are celebrated for their precision and succinctness. Ludovic labors lovingly over his first compositions, revising, polishing, searching for exactly the right word. By contrast, his novel, *The Death Wish*, is written with steadily decreasing control; the words "poured from his pen in disordered confusion."

As Ludovic's prose style changes, his character seems to change, too. The combined efforts of Sir Ralph Brompton and the British military have made him a man without a context—he no longer fits anywhere. He changes from a man who can pass among either officers or other ranks to one who can pass as neither. He becomes progressively alienated and childlike, first shifting his affection to a puppy whom he addresses in babytalk and then shifting his location to Castello Crouchback, that bastion of prewar comfort and isolation.

As Ludovic becomes more romantic, more alienated, and more public (his novel is a great success), Guy becomes more realistic, more sure of his context, and more private. Following his father's death, and armed with his father's precept "Quantitative judgments don't apply," Guy begins to develop feelings of fellowship of a kind that can survive in the modern world. For him, fellowship will be centered on the church and the family; that is, it will be at once inclusive and exclusive. When de Souza advises him that "Now's the time to forget we're Jews and simply remember we are anti-fascist," Guy replies, "I can't feel like that about Catholics." At last he has come to feel at home in his religion.

He also comes to feel at home with his family. When he returns to Broome, leaving Castello Crouchback to Ludovic, he marries the Catholic girl of a recusant family (Charles Plessington, her father, was the eligible Catholic man Angela should have married) whom he should have married in the first place. Although the baby Gervase is Virginia's and Trimmer's child biologically, he is the son and heir of the Crouchback family, of which Guy is the head. With a Catholic wife and child, living on ancestral land (even though it is in the Lesser House), Guy is no longer an exile from his family.

Guy's attendance at the reunion of the X Commando at Bellamy's also suggests that he has learned to balance his tendency toward withdrawal with carefully limited fellowship. The narrator is at pains to point out repeatedly that withdrawal is a family trait. But Waugh is loath to call it by a single name. In Ivo, withdrawal was madness and so more to be pitied than censured. In Tony Box-Bender, it may be vocation and so to be admired. In Guy, however, it was spiritual weakness and so to be overcome.

Guy's movement toward the private, then, is combined with what appears to be a movement outward, a rejection of withdrawal. This combination may sound like a contradiction, but it is really a paradoxical manifestation of the balance Guy has achieved and learned to maintain. Being private need not imply being alone; it may simply imply a closely circumscribed realm of activity. For example, for Guy and his family to return to Broome where Dominica manages the home farm is rather like Candide learning to cultivate his garden. The selling of Castello Crouchback and the decision not to go often to London indicate Guy's commitment to participation in a small, private world.

As the preceding discussion suggests, buildings are central to the establishment of values in the war trilogy. The technique in *Men at Arms* differs from that of *Brideshead Revisited* in that Waugh does not give as much close attention to architecture and decoration here as he did in the earlier novel, yet he uses the descriptions of buildings in a telling way.

Despite the prime position of the opening scene being given to Castello Crouchback, an older, colder, and less voluptuous structure makes strong claims as a central image in *Men at Arms*. It is Broome, the ancestral home of the Crouchbacks. This center of the family is also a center of English Catholicism, never having been without a priest, even in the worst days of Catholic persecution, and having descended through the male line since the days of Henry I (i.e., the twelfth century). Broome has now become too expensive for Guy's aging father to maintain, but he has not sold it. Rather, he rents it to a convent so that "the sanctuary lamp still burn[s] at Broome as of old."

Throughout his lifetime, Gervase Crouchback has sold off parts of the estate, not only because it did not make money but because an outlay was required every year whether it was making money or not. This diminution of the estate established in

Men at Arms is mirrored in the description of the church at Broome in *Unconditional Surrender* when Mr. Crouchback is buried. The church, which was originally Catholic, was given over to the Church of England, except for one aisle and the cemetery, which belong to the lord of the manor. Thus the Catholics have been edged out of their rightful stations but they cannot be completely expunged.

In *Men at Arms*, Broome is emptied of all the secular trophies of the long years. But despoiling the earthly trophies of the family—the dingy carpets, the stuffed bear, the weapons that used to hang on the walls of the great hall—does not change Broome from a Catholic center to something else; for whatever happens, the sanctuary lamp still burns.

This symbol of the continuity of English Catholicism explains why it is so important for Guy and Domenica to live at Broome at the end of the battle. Catholicism and the meaning it brings to existence are at the center of their lives. Their return to Broome is an indication that the faith and its community of souls are there to provide meaning in a world that has become sad, dark, and without honor.

The second building of major thematic importance in the trilogy is Guy's Italian castle home. The novel opens with a short sketch of the arrival in Italy of Guy's grandparents, Gervase and Hermione, and of their creation of Castello Crouchback. This initial sequence is important in establishing two themes: It likens the Catholic Church to an army ("The City, lapped now by the tide of illustrious converts, still remembered with honour its old companions in arms") and it establishes that this is a novel, indeed a trilogy, about love—conjugal love, family love, love of country, love of friends, love of God. Thus the title, *Men at Arms* refers both to members of the Catholic Church and to the men of the modern military. The presence of Gervase and Hermione serves to establish a record of the possibility in an earlier, simpler age of the kind of perfect happiness that Waugh seems to suggest is no longer possible. The severity of

Guy's spiritual malaise is illustrated vividly by the fact that even at Castello Crouchback, that "place of joy and love," he is unhappy. And he believes that his unhappiness is a result of the "Modern Age."

There are ways in which Guy's analysis of his problem is correct. It may be that the social order of a democracy is inferior to that of an aristocracy. It may be that alliances based on secular and political grounds are inferior to those based on religious grounds. However, one cannot choose not to live in the Modern Age, and it is part of Guy's spiritual task to discover what of value remains in this wasteland.

Castello Crouchback, on the other hand, passes out of the family in *Unconditional Surrender* and Guy reports to Box-Bender that he has sold it to Ludovic, that erstwhile classicist author of *Pensees* who finally shows his true bent by writing a richly romantic novel—"Angela read it. She said it was tosh." Angela was probably right. Although Castello Crouchback seems to present an ideal in the opening scenes of the trilogy when it is used to symbolize the near perfection of human love, the process of the trilogy shows how much more one should value the love of God and God's love for mankind, particularly Catholic mankind, as symbolized by Broome.

Waugh is particularly effective in loading Broome with meaning without ever really showing the reader anything about life there. The experience is a dream as heaven is a dream. There is almost no detail of life at Broome available to the reader, nor, for that matter, of life at Castello Crouchback. But there are domestic details in abundance regarding the Halberdier barracks, Kut-al-Imara House, Matchet, the X Commando hotel in Scotland, and so on. This attention to detail in describing the unsatisfactory aspects of life indicates how deeply Waugh is concerned with the importance of exile in the war trilogy. It is also an indication of the weakness of satire—it is much more fun to write about what is wrong than about what is right.

Waugh uses the Halberdier barracks to symbolize the progress of Guy's relationship with the corps. As a probationary officer, he sees the barracks in a rosy and romantic glow. There is a fireplace in the anteroom to the mess hall in which a fire glows cheerily. Above the fireplace is an oil-painting of the "unbroken square of Halberdiers in the desert," a clear call to glory. The tables are set with silver candelabra, and the beer is served in silver goblets. Furthermore, the mess hall is fully populated, for the Halberdiers dine comfortably.

In *Officers and Gentlemen*, when Guy returns to the barracks after Apthorpe's death, his attitude toward the military has changed, and so has the home of the Halberdiers. No longer warm, cozy, and romantic, the anteroom to the mess hall has been stripped:

A dark rectangle over the fireplace marked the spot where "The Unbroken Square" had hung; the bell from the Dutch frigate, the Afridi banner, the gilt idol from Burma, the Napoleonic cuirasses, the Ashanti drum, the loving cup from Barbados, Tipu Sultan's musket, all were gone.

Furthermore, the fireplace is cold, the rations are poor, and the mess hall is deserted. Like Brideshead, the barracks has been desecrated by the modern age in arms; it is now as empty as Guy's life.

Kut-al-Imara House, to which the probationary officers are sent when they leave the regimental barracks, is used almost exclusively to indict the military and to prefigure Guy's inevitable disenchantment with the system. Waugh describes features of life at Kut-al-Imara House in such a way as to ensure that the reader will compare the experience to that of the barracks: the officers are surly and unhelpful; the tableware consists of enamel plates and mugs and cutlery of some anonymous grey metal, surely not silver; the food is colorless and unappetizing: "margarine, sliced bread, huge bluish potatoes and a kind of drab galantine." The kindest thing one can say about it is that it is depressing. To compare it to the barracks is to see that Guy's love affair with the army is bound to end.

Waugh has introduced another, subtler indictment of the military to his description of Kut-al-Imara House through his choices of names for the sleeping rooms in the boy's dormitories. Like Kut-al-Imara itself, Paschendael, Loos, Wipers (Ypres), and Anzac are all the names of World War I battles. Further, they are all battles in which errors in strategic analysis at the highest levels led to the loss of thousands of lives. What these battles have in common is not that they were losses, but that even the victories among them were far too costly to bear. Thus Kut-al-Imara House itself speaks of the immovable bureaucracy, the confusion, the lack of focus that Waugh finds characteristic of the military establishment.

Throughout *Men at Arms* Waugh's continuing concern with the uses and misuses of language is evident. As the world of the novel is a world without much disinterested love, it is also a world of little communication—language fails to carry meaning or, worse, it misrepresents meaning. This theme is established in the first pages of the novel where Guy goes to confession: he speaks Italian well, we are told, but without nuances. Such language, the reader infers, is suitable only for the uncomplicated issues in life, and none of Guy's life is uncomplicated. However, he pretends it is by refusing to think of the nuances. For what is important, that is, for Guy's spiritual state, there are no words.

That there are no words is brought home by the fact that Guy's attempts to initiate or continue conversations on religious or spiritual subjects are consistently failures. People, even well-meaning people, simply do not understand what he is talking about much of the time. For example, when Guy explains to his nephew Tony that "one wants to be with one's own people in war time," Tony's dismissive response is, "Can't see it." Or, more to the point, when Guy tries to talk religion with the chaplain at the guest night dinner, nothing very good happens:

". . .Do you agree," he asked earnestly, "that the Supernatural Order is not something added to the Natural Order, like music or painting, to make everyday life more tolerable? It *is* everyday life. The supernatural is real; what we call 'real' is a mere shadow, a passing fancy. Don't you agree, Padre?"

The import of such an insight to Guy is clear—he is struggling toward a way to make order out of the chaotic modern world and the only way to do that is to say that the disorderly, the chaotic, which dominates his life at the time, is less real than the spiritual or "Supernatural." But the chaplain can only respond, like the foreign editor to Lord Copper, "Up to a point."

Throughout, the novel is marked by various failures of language in many forms and contexts. People switch radios on, looking for information about the war, but nothing is to be learned. Guy's brother-in-law, Arthur Box-Bender, advises Guy to sign on with the BBC who are "keen to collect foreign language speakers . . . for monitoring and propaganda and that sort of rot." That is, they need them to further the misuse of language.

The bureaucratic nonsense of the Box-Bender types also appears in the letters Guy writes to apply for various postings and in the nonsensical replies he receives. He writes begging letters beginning "I hope you remember as I do . . ." or "I am sure I ought not to know, but I *do* know that Alex is Someone Very Important" and he receives "I'll put you on our list and see you're notified as soon as anything turns up." And he knows that really means don't call us, we'll call you.

Even within families there is an inability to communicate. Tony Box-Bender jokes about collecting an "M.C. and a nice neat wound," which devastates his mother who knows there is no such thing. Tony, Angela, and Guy agree to go to church, and their very talking about it discomfits Arthur Box-Bender who manages to "look self-conscious, as he still did, always, when religious practices were spoken of." Even, and perhaps especially, the letters written home from the front illustrate the point. It is not, Waugh is at pains to explain, a simple matter of the educated versus the ignorant, it is rather a case of the feeling versus the modern and thus unfeeling:

Guy remembered the immense boredom of censoring those letters home. Here and there one came across a man who through some oddity of upbringing had escaped the state schools. These wrote with wild phonetic mis-spellings straight from the heart. The rest strung together cliches which he supposed somehow communicated some exchange of affection and need.

If personal communication is problematic in *Men at Arms*, communication within institutions is worse. Guy's life in the military, which he loves, is a series of disasters and near-disasters brought on by failures to communicate. From his first day in the barracks, language complicates things. Having learned how to say "Here's how" to a chum over a drink, Guy is immediately caught short by the benevolent Major Tickeridge who has to point out that "junior officers aren't supposed to drink in the ante-room before lunch." There are several delicious ironies here including (1) Guy and Apthorpe are not the "youngsters" for whom the rule is intended and (2) it's all right if they drink in the billiards room. The language of the rule is fairly clear, but even as it is explicated by the most admirable of men and officers, it becomes nonsense. This passage, however, is a mere presage of things to come.

Failure to communicate is also the problem when Guy's training group is first moved from the barracks to Kut-al-Imara House. He and seven others, having followed the instructions of their transfer orders to the letter, arrive late. Although they have travelled for hours and have not eaten, they are treated unsympathetically by the officer who checks them in. His most comforting observation is, "Well, that's the army all over, isn't it?"

Waugh also uses the failure to communicate theme to provide one of the best comic sketches of Apthorpe's monomania: the episode of Apthorpe and the signalers. In that it is funny when the newly minted company commander sets out to make quite sure that the signalers fail to communicate, the intent is purely humorous; but at the same time, Apthorpe's success in disrupting the world and in preventing it from functioning in an orderly way makes the passage satiric. When the brigadier orders an exercise to see if the signalers "can work their instruments," the language becomes religious: "there arose from dawn till noon a monotonous, liturgical incantation: . . . 'Hullo Nan, Hullo Nan. Report my signals. . . .' Throughout the chill forenoon the prayer rose to the disdainful gods."

And then there are the cases where the message simply does not get through, for example when Guy nearly has two officers from the Seventh Loamshires assassinated or when he takes his company out on a night-training excercise and nearly gets left behind by the rest of the brigade. The problem may reside in the person of Sarum-Smith, but he is only an incarnation of the modern spirit in which sloth and disorder are paramount because no sense of personal honor or shame exists to resist them. Furthermore, these episodes of failure to communicate are not trivial. They may be funny, as when Guy sends his sergeant down to the beach to cover the visiting officers with a machine gun, but they are life threatening as well. Guy reflects that the officers of the Loamshires "were as close to death" on that bathing beach as they had ever been before.

The theme of this failure to communicate is repeated throughout the trilogy and provides a consistent comic touch whenever it is sounded. For example, one of the latest recapitulations comes when Guy receives the telegram informing him of the birth of Virginia's son:

Next morning he received in clear: *P/302/B Personal for Crouchback. Message begins Virginia gave bath son today both well. . . .*

"Query 'bath,'" Guy told his signaller.

Three days later he received: *Personal for Crouchback. Our P/203/B for bath read birch.* . .

"Query 'birch.'"

At length he received: *For birch read birth. repeat birth. Congratulations Cape.*

The centrality of language to experience is asserted and reasserted in *Unconditional Surrender.* Here among the Yugoslavs, Guy is linguistically disenfranchised. He can communicate with the partisans only through an interpreter whose commitment is to the Yugoslavs rather than to the British, so the translation is suspect. Among the Jews whose languages vary, he can speak only to Madame Kanyi, and their ability to communicate without an interpreter leads to her death, for it makes her suspect in the eyes of the partisans.

Among the Yugoslavs, he can communicate only with the parish priest, and then in Latin, which allows him to provide a mass for Virginia and lends support to the universality of the Latin mass of which Waugh was a strong supporter. This point is made and then undercut in the same paragraph when the interpreter, Bakic, follows Guy to the church and Guy bristles at his presence:

"What do you want?"
"I thought maybe you want to talk to somebody."
"I don't require an interpreter when I say my prayers," Guy said.
But later he wondered, did he?

The orthodox answer is yes, but the "interpreter" is not Bakic but Christ.

6

Innocence and Experience

The Ordeal of Gilbert Pinfold

When *The Ordeal of Gilbert Pinfold* was published in 1957, three years after the ordeal of Evelyn Waugh had provided the stimulus for the work, the reaction of the critics was mixed. It is as if reviewers had a very difficult time approving of Waugh's attempt at anything new. Some reviewers praised him for being brave enough to try an autobiographical novel; others deplored his doing so; one took the occasion to subject the author to a not very subtle psychological analysis.

Waugh consistently drew on his own experiences and those of his friends in the construction of his novels. He was cheerful about admitting that he did so, and he often spoke candidly about the sources of his themes, plots and characters. But he did not simply transcribe life into novels. Life is sometimes as absurd as it appears in a Waugh novel, but it is seldom as well structured, and Waugh's genius was his ability to weave the odd strands of his experience into a fabric so carefully designed that the odd strands themselves seem to have been planned. The curious reader who looks to Waugh's letters and diaries will find situations, anecdotes, even phrases that are repeated almost verbatim in the novels; the difference is that the novels are more coherent and ultimately more joyous than his life. But at no time was he as close to transcribing experience throughout an entire work as he was in *The Ordeal of Gilbert Pinfold*.

In the late winter of 1953, Waugh began to have a great

deal of difficulty separating illusion from reality. The first trace of this problem in his letters is a postcard he sent to Lord Kinross asking whether Kinross could testify that a washstand given to Waugh as a gift had originally had a "serpentine bronze pipe which led from the dragon's mouth to the basin."[1] It had not, but Waugh could recall the missing part with such clarity that he could not believe he was mistaken. He harassed the movers, the former owner, and finally the giver of the gift before he could be persuaded that he had never seen the tap he imagined in this washstand.

After Christmas, his physical health deteriorated, too. He was miserable, suffering from "first a cold & then agonising rheumatism,"[2] so he did what he had always done—he booked a tour to the sunny side of the winter world. He had not been out of England long when his wife began to receive disturbing letters about his "persecution mania" and "malevolent telepathy."[3] At his worst he was convinced that "everything I say or think or read is read aloud by the group of psychologists whom I met in the ship."[4] His wife persuaded him to fly home and to consult an "alienist," and when he gave up the chloral he had been using as a sleeping draft, he seemed to recover. Still, the episode, which he described as one in which "the reason remains strenuously active but the information on which it acts is delusory,"[5] shook his confidence and made him feel that an irrevocable mental collapse was imminent. The reviewers seemed to sense his fear.

The *Spectator* observed that "the present reviewer, who has no claim to speak for the British lunatic, found 'The Ordeal' moderately interesting, almost entirely unfunny, and a little embarrassing."[6] Philip Toynbee, writing for the *Observer*, found it "very hard to say whether [*Pinfold*] is a good book or not." But he did see that "it is a book which seems to suggest that Mr. Waugh has shifted gear and has begun to explore depths of experience which were previously beyond his reach—or at least beyond his desire."[7] The most vicious review, however, was by

J. B. Priestley in the *New Statesman*. Priestley seemed compelled to attack Waugh's personal life under guise of reviewing the book, and his article "What Was Wrong with Pinfold" was a thinly disguised discussion of what was wrong with Evelyn Waugh. Priestley averred that Pinfold/Waugh's nervous collapse was a result of his trying to live a double life. The argument went something like this: Waugh is an artist pretending to be a member of the Catholic landed gentry. With such a distance between reality and illusion, Priestley found it not very surprising that Waugh had suffered a nervous collapse. In fact, he thought that the only surprise would be if it did not happen again, and soon. [8] In all, the review was more a review of Waugh's character than of the novel; in addition, it was a cruel attack on the author. To have said that the book was a failure was the reviewer's prerogative; to say that it failed because its author had been mentally ill and that he would soon be mentally ill again was not.

Tasteless as his rhetorical strategy had been, Priestley was exactly right in seeing that *The Ordeal of Gilbert Pinfold* was an autobiographical novel. The opening chapter, in which Mr. Pinfold is introduced, provides a precise description of Waugh in his fifties. Pinfold is "devoted to a wife many years younger than himself" and has numerous children whom he can just barely afford to educate. He used to travel regularly, but in recent years he has not. He served honorably in the war but has not tried to use that experience to enter any public forum. He and his family live in a remote village and have no close neighbors. He is not very social. He is also not very modern: "He abhorred plastics, Picasso, sunbathing, and jazz—everything in fact that had happened in his own lifetime."

At the opening of the novel, Pinfold is ill and finding it difficult to work. He drinks excessively and takes chloral to help him sleep. In addition, his joints and muscles ache, and his drafty house does little to comfort him. Thus, he decides to sail to the sunny south to recuperate. He books a cabin on a ship called

Caliban (after Shakespeare's monster in *The Tempest*). Although the captain, the crew, and the passengers seem to the reader to be polite and innocuous, Pinfold feels that the air around him is filled with intrigue. He imagines slights; he overhears conversations critical of his behavior and his novels; he thinks he hears an embarrassing interview between an evangelical minister and a straying member of his flock; he suffers through a rehearsal by a jazz ensemble; and he overhears two incidents in which sailors are injured or killed and their officers fail to help or protect them. Eventually, one of his persecutors falls in love with him and seems to attempt to seduce him; she then fails to keep their assignation. Although Pinfold is convinced that he is being harassed by "psychologists" from the BBC, he determines that the best way to thwart them is to return home. When he arrives in England, his wife recalls him to reality by pointing out that his analysis of what has happened simply cannot be true. He understands immediately, is returned to reason, and leaves London for home with his wife. When he consults his doctor, the doctor diagnoses a case of poisoning, but Pinfold continues to believe that he has won a moral victory. Most important, he is again able to write.

The novel is circular in structure, concluding with Mr. Pinfold's beginning to write the story the reader has just finished reading. Within the circular outline, it is hard to say that the novel is particularly highly structured. The events on the ship, although well presented individually, seem episodic rather than hierarchical. That is, it is hard to see why the jazz music and the dog should precede the evangelical religious service, for example. But if one looks not so much at the incidents as at Pinfold's responses to them, one sees a progression that does help in appreciating the interior shape of the novel.

When Pinfold leaves England, he is almost entirely passive. This is a great difficulty for him, because as a writer he thinks of himself as a maker of things, and that requires action. But

Mr. Pinfold does not write; instead he feels the need "of longer periods of sleep." His church exhorts him to become involved in social causes, but he cannot even make the effort to go to mass. He wants to avoid his enthusiastic neighbor, whom he calls "the Bruiser," but he can't make himself get up and leave the room, even to avoid having to hear about the miraculous healing powers of the Bruiser's electronic box. The only thing he can make himself do before he leaves England is visit his mother. Although the visit is "not a success," at least it is made; and that alone is enough to signify the central importance of family in this short work.

Pinfold's passivity continues on board the ship. When he begins to hear voices, he avoids them by taking one of his gray pills and lying down to read. When the mad evangelist begins to work on Billy, Pinfold leaves his cabin to avoid overhearing the interview. As long as he continues to read and imagine, he continues to feel ill and lame. It is not until the episode in which the captain and Goneril torture one of the stewards to death that Pinfold is incited to action. Determined to "stop this outrage at once," Pinfold "lurches" out of his bunk and discovers that his rheumatism is gone. That is, as soon as he wants to be able to move, he can do so. It is also significant that it is the pressure of physical assault that allows him to overcome his physical infirmities. The first is the case of the tortured steward; later the threat of attack by Fosker and the other hooligans causes him to prepare to be physically brave.

The second symptom of Pinfold's distress is his wish for solitude. Although he is lonely, he wants to be left alone. This is the significance of the introduction of his friends in the early pages of the novel. His old friends are important to him, but he has begun to feel that they love him less than they used to, and he has made no new friends. On the ship, he doesn't want to be with people, but he does not have the strength of mind to take the action needed to be allowed, for example, to dine alone.

He feels that he is obliged to undertake social intercourse even though he is not interested. He finds that he cannot be alone without feeling that he is excluded.

The voices are an excellent image of his predicament, because they talk to him and speak what he is thinking whether he tries to snub them or not. He is unable to exert any control over the voices until he chooses to rejoin his fellows by announcing his intention to dine at the captain's table again. At that point the voices become an undertone, only intermittently breaking through his real conversations. However, it is not until he is able to acknowledge that he has control over his privacy, that is, not until he is willing to say "I can't talk to the Bruiser" and then do something about it, that we feel sure of his recovery.

The third sign that something is wrong with Pinfold is that "His strongest tastes were negative." That is, he has become increasingly exclusionary in his outlook, tending to ignore or reject "everything in fact that had happened in his own lifetime." In short, Pinfold's recent history is one of failure to engage the world. He ignores his village duties; he and his wife no longer socialize with neighbors; his religion is a "slight but perceptible barrier"; he is withdrawing from his old friends and not making any new ones; he is not interested in anything new; he has stopped writing; and he has even begun to deny half of his personality. Whole areas of his experience have dried up. The only relationship that remains completely vital is that with his wife.

In essence, then, Pinfold is a true exile; he is cut off from everything. He is separated from his neighbors by his religion (here as in *Men at Arms* the church does not provide a sense of community), and by his own lack of interest in village affairs. He is cut off from friends and family by the persona that has become his personality. The voyage provides a metaphor for his estrangement from family and friends, an estrangement that is at once painful and necessary, for without it he cannot be an artist.

Pinfold's wife is not a very realistic character in the novel, but then no character other than Pinfold himself is really convincing here. Despite her lack of roundness, however, she is important to the development of the novel. Although she actually appears in the novel only in the opening and closing pages, her influence is felt in nearly every episode. She is introduced early as "a wife many years younger than himself" to whom Pinfold is devoted. He notes with sorrow the anxiety she feels over her fields and resents on her behalf the trickery of her tenant, Hill. He feels that she gets on better with his mother than he does. When he overhears one of his voices saying that the mysterious dark man has been sent by his wife to keep an eye on him, his first response is that she will enjoy the joke. When he thinks Margaret's mother has offered Margaret to him, he replies that he has a wife whom he loves. He writes to her of his suspicions and she, in effect, rescues him from his voices by persuading him to return to England and by being a person against whom the voices cannot turn him. Even at their strongest, and even after they have made him doubt the captain, the crew, the other passengers, his old friend James Lance, and the BBC, the voices cannot make him doubt his wife. Pinfold's absolute confidence in his wife and her love is his greatest spiritual strength and is ultimately responsible for recalling him to life.

In addition to his wife, Pinfold has absolute confidence in his reason. Throughout the voyage, he solves the puzzle of the voices again and again, never doubting his own ability to do so. He is acutely aware of the contradictions in what the voices have to say, and he sees those contradictions as evidence that the voices do not know what they are talking about, but he does not see the contradictions in his own behavior as he advances one hypothesis after another. He continues to the very end to trust his reason and to appeal to it; the last, unanswered question he raises is an appeal to reason: "If I was supplying all the information to the Angels, why did I tell them such a lot of rot?" Reason, we see, is not as powerful a force as love because reason cannot help him, but love can. However, both reason and love seem to be necessary for the creation of art.

Finally, along with love of family and reason, religion plays an important role in Pinfold's progress. The pattern of religious withdrawal and recommitment in the novel is clear and consistent with the pattern of the voyage out and back. Just before leaving England, when he is at his most infirm, Pinfold misses mass. Weak and sick his first night on the ship, he takes his medicines before retiring, but neglects his prayers. When he begins to say his prayers, three days later, two important things happen. The affectionate Margaret becomes progressively central among the voices, and Pinfold makes the decision to discuss his harassment with the Captain. Whether changing from the captain's table to another and from his original cabin to another is important or not, the fact that Pinfold has a discussion with a real person and takes action of some sort is important.

After the prayers of the third day, Pinfold again stops saying his prayers because "the familiar, hallowed words provoked a storm of blasphemous parody from Goneril." When he arrives in Colombo, his destination, he attends mass for the first time since before leaving England. This appears to be significant, since only Margaret follows him "into the dusky, crowded interior" of the church. However, it is not Pinfold's attending mass that makes Mr. Angel take up a defensive stance; rather, reaching "Christendom" puts Pinfold in control. Between Rome and London he makes the brave decision to confront his tormentors rather than to compromise with them. Making that decision to do rather than not do, to speak rather than to remain silent, and to take action rather than to remain passive is his victory. Clearly, the novel suggests that the decision has to be made in a Christian context, but Christianity alone is not enough.

The most immediate influence on Pinfold's return to clarity

of vision, then, is not the church but his wife. She takes him by the hand and points out that the elaborate rational explanations he has developed for this most irrational series of events are flawed. Mr. Angel has not been out of the country, and no invention such as Pinfold has described exists. And the moment she pronounces the words and, more important, he believes her, he is cured. It is the mutual trust between man and wife that is more immediately important than any other single fact of Pinfold's life: "This he knew was the final truth. He was alone with his wife." That is, he is simultaneously alone and in company, the state of balance he has been seeking.

At the end of his adventure, Pinfold is back where he began, but with a difference. The house, we are told, is "cold as ever," but Mr. Pinfold is now able to live there. He can act to choose his surroundings and his companions, and he no longer avoids the library, which means that he no longer avoids his art. Aroused from his passivity, he can once again assume the role of a maker of literary artifacts. He is indeed reborn.

Like so many other Waugh novels, the structure takes the reader out and back: Pinfold begins at home, in a cold house, wanting to avoid the Bruiser and his box, and he finishes at home, in a cold house, wanting to avoid the Bruiser and his box. But this has been a voyage of discovery for Pinfold, and no one would argue that Gilbert has come back the same man he was when he left. There is clearly progress in *The Ordeal of Gilbert Pinfold*, and that progress takes place in all the important areas of Pinfold's life: in his relations with his family, with his art, and with his religion.

7

A Man of Style

Sadly, the successful re-entry into life symbolized by Gilbert Pinfold's recovery was not fully realized in Waugh's own case. He continued to write but the premonition that he had only one or two good books left in him proved to be well-founded. After *Pinfold* he wrote little fiction—*Unconditional Surrender*, a recension of the war trilogy called *Sword of Honour*, and *Basil Seal Rides Again*. However, he also completed a life of Ronald Knox and one more travel book, *A Tourist in Africa*. In addition, he undertook a three-volume autobiography but was unable to continue past the first volume, which was entitled *A Little Learning*.

A valedictory quality pervades Waugh's last works. In *Basil Seal Rides Again*, for example, he brings the no-longer-young Basil back for one more hurrah, but provides him with a willful grown-up daughter and a propensity to gout. In the revision of the war trilogy, he reconsiders his early generosity in giving Guy and Domenica children of their own and makes the son of Virginia and Trimmer the only heir to the Crouchback estate.[1] In general, he saw ahead for England and Catholicism an uninviting, dull and deteriorating condition.

One hopes that despite his despondency, Waugh had an appreciation of his great success as a man of letters, for indeed his achievement was remarkable. For example, during his lifetime his works were regularly translated into foreign languages all across Europe. His novels have never been out of print and are even now, more than twenty years after his death, available in collected editions both in Britain and in the United States.

His readership is so wide that any new comic-satiric novelist of talent is sure to be described as "the best since Evelyn Waugh" or "in the tradition of Evelyn Waugh."

In addition to remaining popular with the reading public, Waugh commands a great deal of respect from the scholarly community. His diaries were published in 1976, his letters in 1980, and a collection of his journalism in 1983. As he foresaw, his papers have been purchased by the "yanks" and are among the more important assets of the Humanities Research Center of the University of Texas. Most important of all, he is generally accepted as the finest prose stylist of his generation and perhaps of the twentieth century.

For Waugh, style was always a central aesthetic concern. From the word through the sentence, the paragraph and the chapter, to the overall structure, he was as meticulous as the furniture maker he had once tried to be in choosing just the right element and fitting it carefully into its proper place. Even in the early days as a writer and critic, he demonstrated in his letters, diaries, and articles a concern for structure, that is for style in its largest sense.

In reviewing Cyril Connolly's *Enemies of Promise* in 1938, for example, Waugh suggested that a real writer's gifts, as opposed to those of a critic, are "architectural." He went on to explain, "I believe that what makes a writer, as distinct from a clever and cultured man who can write, is an added energy and breadth of vision which enables him to conceive and complete a structure."[2] The architectural analogy also conveys the notion that books are objects which are made, crafted perhaps, in the same sense that buildings are made.

In a similar vein, he wrote to Nancy Mitford, congratulating her on the success of her *Voltaire in Love*:

> You write so deceptively frivolously that one races on chuckling from page to page without noticing the solid structure. Perhaps because I've just finished writing a biography myself . . . I can now

realize what an achievement of research, selection & arrangement you apparently effortlessly performed.[3]

In addition to illustrating the centrality of a strong structure to Waugh's aesthetic, this remark reveals his craftsmanlike attitude toward the process by which strong structures are made. They are, he asserts, the products of "selection and arrangement," not of genius, instinct, or insight. In the review of *Enemies of Promise*, he had expanded upon that very point, saying,

Writing is an art which exists in a time sequence; each sentence and each page is dependent on its predecessors and successors; a sentence which [the critic] admires may owe its significance to another fifty pages distant. I beg Mr. Connolly to believe that even quite popular writers take great trouble sometimes in this matter.[4]

For Waugh, then, the architectural implications of style were of primary importance. This fact is reflected in the careful structuring of his own works, most of which tend to be circular or based on a life or a journey. Structure, however, was not the only important aspect of style for Waugh. He was also extremely conscious of the demands of style in matters of vocabulary, diction and grammar. Although his private utterances in letters, diaries, and conversation could be slangy and even obscene at times, in his public utterances (his books, articles, and interviews) he aspired to a correctness based on classical models. In an essay on "Literary Style in England and America," Waugh explained how his style and that of his contemporaries developed:

All English boys, of the kind who are now writers, learned Latin from the age of nine. Very few girls did. The boys did not become ripe scholars, but they acquired a basic sense of the structure of language which never left them; they learned to scan quite elaborate metres; they learned to compose Latin verses of a kind themselves. Little girls learned French and were praised for idiomatic volubility.[5]

For the voluble, the imprecise, the repetitive, and the slangy, Waugh had little tolerance. He believed that the English language was the richest in the world and that it was capable of producing such delicate shades of meaning that imprecision was unacceptable. Thus when Stephen Spender announced in his *World Within World* that he was "impatient with that side of writing which consists in balancing a sentence, choosing the exact word, writing grammatically even," Waugh was plainly irritated. His comment: "Why, one asks, does Mr. Spender write at all?"[6]

He was similarly disappointed, although much more gentle in expressing it, when he took Nancy Mitford to task for using "aggravate" to mean "annoy." He refers her to the *Oxford English Dictionary* and notes, "your 'aggravate' is 7th of the meanings and the authorities are negligible except when it is used conversationally in fiction by people of low education."[7] His punctiliousness on these issues resulted in acute embarrassment when he caught himself in a mistake. For example, he wrote to Ann Fleming complaining, "I wrote a review in great haste for *Sunday Times* saying 'please correct mistakes'. They left 'marriage blanche' for 'mariage blanc'. Very humiliating particularly as the point of the review was mocking D. Cecil's bad grammar."[8]

Although one may feel that there is a self-congratulatory quality to Waugh's railing about the failures of contemporaries to the use of the language properly, it is clear that he was as hard on himself as on others in these matters. For Waugh, style was not only the backbone of his aesthetic creed, it was his only means of protection from the boredom, depression and self-doubt that were his lifelong weaknesses. As early as 1955, he formulated an explanation of the importance of style for his life and his work, writing,

One thing I hold as certain, that a writer, if he is to develop, must concern himself more and more with Style. He cannot hope to interest the majority of his readers in his progress. It is his own interest that is at stake. Style alone can keep him from being bored with his own work.[9]

By following his own advice he not only kept his psychological demons at bay, but transformed himself from a popular novelist to a serious aesthetician, and his novels from simple best-sellers to touchstones of twentieth-century fiction.

Notes

1. BIOGRAPHY

1. Evelyn Waugh, *The Ordeal of Gilbert Pinfold* (1957. reprint New York: Penguin Books, 1962), pp. 9–10.

2. Christopher Sykes, *Evelyn Waugh: A Biography* (London: William Collins Sons, 1975), p. 449.

3. Evelyn Waugh, *A Little Learning* (Boston: Little, Brown and Company, 1964), p. 27.

4. Ibid., p. 33.

5. Evelyn Waugh, "Fan-Fare," *The Essays, Articles and Reviews of Evelyn Waugh*, ed. Donat Gallagher (Boston: Little, Brown and Company, 1984), p. 301.

6. Waugh, *A Little Learning*, p. 62.

7. Ibid., p. 68.

8. Ibid., p. 96.

9. Ibid.

10. Evelyn Waugh, *The Diaries of Evelyn Waugh*, ed. Michael Davie (Boston: Little, Brown and Company, 1976), p. 26.

11. Ibid., p. 29.

12. Waugh, *A Little Learning*, p. 148.

13. Waugh, *Diaries*, p. 9.

14. Evelyn Waugh, *The Letters of Evelyn Waugh*, ed. Mark Amory (London: Weidenfeld & Nicolson, 1980; reprint New York: Penguin Books, 1982), p. 19.

15. Waugh, *Diaries*, p. 195.

16. Ibid., p. 281.

17. Ibid., p. 282.

18. Waugh, *Letters*, p. 38.

19. Ibid., p. 38.

20. Waugh, *Diaries*, p. 309.

21. See, for example, Sykes, pp. 141–42.

22. Graham Greene, review of *Edmund Campion*, in *Evelyn Waugh: The Critical Heritage*, ed. Martin Stannard (London: Routledge & Kegan Paul, 1984), p. 165.

23. J. A. Kensit, review of *Edmund Campion*, ibid., pp. 166–67.

24. Evelyn Waugh, *Waugh in Abyssinia* (New York: Longmans, Green and Co., 1936), p. 49.

25. Quoted in Sykes, p. 182.

26. Evelyn Waugh, *When the Going Was Good* (Boston: Little, Brown and Company, 1946), p. x.

27. Waugh, *Diaries*, p. 557.

28. Sykes, pp. 238–39.

29. Waugh, *Letters*, p. 196.

30. Ibid., p. 208.

31. Ibid., p. 259.

32. Ibid., p. 312.

33. Ibid., pp. 340–41.

34. Ibid., p. 354.

35. Sykes, p. 355.

36. Waugh, *Letters*, p. 417.

37. Evelyn Waugh, "Awake My Soul! It is a Lord," Gallagher, p. 468.

38. Evelyn Waugh, "Dr. Wodehouse and Mr. Wain," Gallagher, p. 507.

39. Sykes, p. 455.

40. Waugh, *Letters*, p. 631.

41. Ibid., p. 639.

42. Ibid., p. 636.

2. INNOCENTS AT HOME

1. See, for example, A. A. DeVitis, *Roman Holiday: The Catholic Novels of Evelyn Waugh* (New York: Bookman Associates, 1956).

2. Eric Bentley, "The Psychology of Farce," *Let's Get a Divorce! and Other Plays* (New York: Hill and Wang, 1958), p. xix.

3. Gerald Gould, review of *Decline and Fall* in Stannard, p. 81.

4. J. B. Priestley, review of *Decline and Fall* in Stannard, p. 84.

5. Waugh, *Letters*, p. 27.

6. James F. Carens, *The Satiric Art of Evelyn Waugh* (Seattle: University of Washington Press, 1966), p. 11.

7. Bentley, "The Psychology of Farce," p. x.

8. V. S. Pritchett, review of *Vile Bodies* in Stannard, p. 97.

9. Rebecca West, review of *Vile Bodies* in Stannard, p. 106.

10. Ralph Straus, review of *Vile Bodies* in Stannard, p. 95.

11. Arnold Bennett, review of *Vile Bodies* in Stannard, p. 99.

12. Waugh, *Letters*, p. 39.

13. Rebecca West, review of *Vile Bodies* in Stannard, p. 107.

14. Howard Marshall, review of *Black Mischief* in Stannard, p. 127.

15. James Agate, review of *Black Mischief* in Stannard, p. 128.

16. Geoffrey West, review of *Black Mischief* in Stannard, p. 131.

17. Ernest Oldmeadow, review of *Black Mischief* in Stannard, p. 133.

3. INNOCENTS ABROAD

1. Unsigned review of *A Handful of Dust* in Stannard, p. 149.

2. Peter Quennell, review of *A Handful of Dust*, ibid., p. 155.

3. Waugh, *Letters*, p. 88.

4. Ibid.

5. Unsigned review of *Scoop* in Stannard, p. 197.

6. Derek Verschagle, review of *Scoop* in Stannard, p. 200.

7. See, for example, Rupert Croft-Cooke's review and that of John Brophy, ibid., pp. 194 and 198.

8. Alan Pryce-Jones, review of *Put Out More Flags* in Stannard, p. 216.

9. George Dangerfield, review of *Put Out More Flags* in Stannard, p. 217.

10. Waugh, *Letters*, p. 158.

4. THE MORAL CENTER

1. Unsigned review of *Brideshead Revisited* in Stannard, pp. 234 and 236.
2. Henry Reed, review of *Brideshead Revisited* in Stannard, pp. 240–41.
3. V. C. Clinton-Baddeley, review of *Brideshead Revisited* in Stannard, pp. 237–38.
4. John K. Hutchens, review of *Brideshead Revisited* in Stannard, pp. 242.
5. Edmund Wilson, review of *Brideshead Revisited* in Stannard, pp. 245–48.
6. Cyril Connolly, in Stannard, p. 300.
7. John Woodburn, review of *The Loved One* in Stannard, p. 304.
8. Unsigned review of *The Loved One* in Stannard, p. 305.
9. Waugh, *Letters*, p. 265.
10. Ibid., p. 312.
11. John Raymond, review of *Helena* in Stannard, p. 321.
12. Unsigned review of *Helena* in Stannard, p. 323.

5. THE WAR TRILOGY

1. Cyril Connolly, review of *Men at Arms* in Stannard, p. 337.
2. John Raymond, review of *Men at Arms* in Stannard, p. 339.
3. Unsigned review of *Men at Arms* in Stannard, p. 341.
4. Joseph Frank, review of *Men at Arms* in Stannard, p. 347.
5. Waugh, *Letters*, p. 354.
6. Ibid., p. 363.
7. Ibid., p. 366.
8. Ibid., p. 370.
9. Ibid., p. 378.
10. Christopher Sykes, review of *Officers and Gentlemen* in Stannard, p. 367.
11. Cyril Connolly, review of *Officers and Gentlemen* in Stannard, p. 370.
12. Kingsley Amis, review of *Officers and Gentlemen* in Stannard, pp. 372 and 374.

13. Waugh, *Letters*, p. 444.

14. Ibid., p. 445.

15. Waugh, *Diaries*, p. 729.

16. Ibid., p. 727.

17. Kingsley Amis, review of *Unconditional Surrender* in Stannard, p. 422.

18. Philip Toynbee, review of *Unconditional Surrender* in Stannard, p. 437.

19. Cyril Connolly, review of *Unconditional Surrender* in Stannard, p. 430.

20. Bernard Bergonzi, review of *Unconditional Surrender* in Stannard, p. 424.

21. Jeffrey Heath, *The Picturesque Prison: Evelyn Waugh and His Writing* (Kingston and Montreal: McGill-Queen's University Press, 1982), pp. 223–24.

6. INNOCENCE AND EXPERIENCE

1. Waugh, *Letters*, p. 416.

2. Ibid., p. 417.

3. Ibid., pp. 418–19.

4. Ibid., p. 419.

5. Quoted in an unsigned review in Stannard, p. 382, this statement originally appeared on the dust jacket of the novel.

6. Donat O'Donnell, review of *Pinfold* in Stannard, p. 380.

7. Philip Toynbee, review of *Pinfold* in Stannard, pp. 386–87.

8. J. B. Priestley, review of *Pinfold* in Stannard, pp. 387–90.

7. A MAN OF STYLE

1. Waugh, *Letters*, p. 579.

2. Waugh, "Present Discontents," in Gallagher, p. 238.

3. Waugh, *Letters*, p. 521.

4. Waugh, "Present Discontents," in Gallagher, p. 239.

5. Waugh, "Literary Style in England and America," in Gallagher, p. 480.

6. Waugh, "Two Unquiet Lives," in Gallagher, p. 395.

7. Waugh, *Letters*, pp. 591–92.

8. Ibid., p. 626.

9. Waugh, "Literary Style in England and America," in Gallagher, p. 481.

Selected Bibliography

BOOKS BY EVELYN WAUGH

Rossetti, His Life and Works. London: Duckworth, 1928. New York: Dodd, Mead and Co., 1928.

Decline and Fall. London: Chapman and Hall, 1928. New York: Doubleday, Doran, 1929.

Vile Bodies. London: Chapman and Hall, 1930. New York: Cape, Smith, 1930.

Labels: A Mediterranean Journal. London: Duckworth, 1930. U. S. edition: *A Bachelor Abroad: A Mediterranean Journal.* New York: Cape, Smith, 1930.

Remote People. London: Duckworth, 1931. U. S. edition: *They Were Still Dancing.* New York: Farrar and Rinehart, 1932.

Black Mischief. London: Chapman and Hall, 1932. New York: Farrar and Rinehart, 1932.

Ninety-Two Days, The Account of a Tropical Journey Through British Guiana and Part of Brazil. London: Duckworth, 1934. New York: Farrar and Rinehart, 1934.

A Handful of Dust. London: Chapman and Hall, 1934. New York: Farrar and Rinehart, 1934.

Edmund Campion: Jesuit and Martyr. London: Longman, 1935. New York: Sheed and Ward, 1935.

Mr Loveday's Little Outing and Other Sad Stories. London: Chapman and Hall, 1936. Boston: Little, Brown, 1936.

Waugh in Abyssinia. London and New York: Longman, Green and Co., 1936.

Scoop. London: Chapman and Hall, 1938. Boston: Little, Brown, 1938.

Robbery Under Law: The Mexican Object-Lesson. London: Chapman and Hall,

179

1939. U.S. edition: *Mexico: An Object Lesson*. Boston: Little, Brown, 1939.

Put Out More Flags. London: Chapman and Hall, 1942. Boston: Little, Brown, 1942.

Brideshead Revisited: The Sacred and Profane Memories of Captain Charles Ryder. London: Chapman and Hall, 1945. Boston: Little, Brown, 1945.

When the Going Was Good. London: Duckworth, 1946. Boston: Little, Brown, 1945.

Scott-King's Modern Europe. London: Chapman and Hall, 1947. Boston: Little, Brown, 1946.

The Loved One. London: Chapman and Hall, 1948. Boston: Little, Brown, 1948.

Work Suspended and Other Stories Written Before the Second World War. London: Chapman and Hall, 1949.

Helena. London: Chapman and Hall, 1950. Boston: Little, Brown, 1952.

Men at Arms. London: Chapman and Hall, 1952. Boston: Little, Brown, 1952.

The Holy Places. London: Queen Anne Press, 1952.

Love Among the Ruins: A Romance of the New Future. London: Chapman and Hall, 1953.

Officers and Gentlemen. London: Chapman and Hall, 1955. Boston: Little, Brown, 1955.

The Ordeal of Gilbert Pinfold. London: Chapman and Hall, 1957. Boston: Little, Brown, 1957. New York: Penguin Books, 1962.

The Life of the Right Reverend Ronald Knox. London: Chapman and Hall, 1959. U.S. edition: *Monsignor Ronald Knox*. Boston: Little, Brown, 1959.

A Tourist in Africa. London: Chapman and Hall, 1960. Boston: Little, Brown, 1960.

Unconditional Surrender. London: Chapman and Hall, 1961. U.S. edition: *The End of the Battle*. Boston: Little, Brown, 1961.

Basil Seal Rides Again or The Rake's Regress. London: Chapman and Hall, 1963. Boston: Little, Brown, 1963.

A Little Learning. London: Chapman and Hall, 1964. Boston: Little, Brown, 1964.

Sword of Honour. London: Chapman and Hall, 1965. Boston: Little, Brown, 1966.

The Diaries of Evelyn Waugh. Edited by Michael Davie. London: Weidenfeld and Nicolson, 1976.

The Letters of Evelyn Waugh. Edited by Mark Amory. London: Weidenfeld and Nicolson, 1980. New York: Penguin Books, 1982.
The Essays, Articles and Reviews of Evelyn Waugh. Edited by Donat Gallagher. London: Methuen, 1983.

WORKS CONSULTED

Bentley, Eric. "The Psychology of Farce." in *Let's Get a Divorce! and Other
Plays.* New York: Hill and Wang, 1958.

Carens, James F. *The Satiric Art of Evelyn Waugh.* Seattle: University of
Washington Press, 1966.

Cook, William J., Jr. *Masks, Modes and Morals: The Art of Evelyn Waugh.*
Cranbury, N.J.: Fairleigh Dickinson University Press, 1971.

Davis, Jessica Milner. *Farce.* London: Methuen, 1978.

De Vitis, A. A. *Roman Holiday: The Catholic Novels of Evelyn Waugh.* New
York: Bookman Associates, 1956.

Donaldson, Frances. *Evelyn Waugh. Portrait of a Country Neighbor.* London: Weidenfeld and Nicolson, 1967.

Doyle, Paul A. *Evelyn Waugh: A Critical Essay.* Grand Rapids, Mich.:
William B. Eerdmans, 1969.

Frye, Northrop. *Anatomy of Criticism.* Princeton: Princeton University
Press, 1957. New York: Atheneum, 1967.

Greenblatt, Stephen Jay. *Three Modern Satirists: Waugh, Orwell and Huxley.*
New Haven: Yale University Press, 1965.

Heath, Jeffrey. *The Picturesque Prison: Evelyn Waugh and His Writing.* Kingston
and Montreal: McGill-Queen's University Press, 1982.

Lodge, David. *Evelyn Waugh.* New York: Columbia University Press,
1971.

Phillips, Gene D. *Evelyn Waugh's Officers, Gentlemen and Rogues: The Fact
Behind His Fiction.* Chicago: Nelson-Hall, 1975.

Pryce-Jones, David, ed. *Evelyn Waugh and His World.* London: Weidenfeld and Nicolson, 1973.

Stannard, Martin, ed. *Evelyn Waugh: The Critical Heritage.* London: Routledge and Kegan Paul, 1984.

Sykes, Christopher. *Evelyn Waugh: A Biography.* London: William Collins Sons, 1975.

Waugh, Alec. *My Brother Evelyn and Other Profiles.* London: Cassell, 1967.

Index